HASSLE OR HARMONY
Every PARENT'S choice

Hassle or harmony:
every couple's choice

Hroth & Victor Bennett
isbn 0 946139 70 9   £5.95 hardback   1987

Designed to help couples who are thinking of getting married as well as those who are at one of the many different stages of a long term relationship. All organisations interested in strengthening marriage bonds and supporting the role of the family will find it useful — for both students and clientele.

The book takes a fresh look at the kind of commitments couples make. It offers ways to reduce tension by better communication and by negotiation. A range of stressful situations drawn from real life are used as examples.

Where breakdown has occurred, practical advice is given on how to adapt to 'single' life, the approach to a possible second marriage, and how to deal with being a step parent. There is a section on how to lessen hassle for and by grandparents.

The value of these ideas has been proven by many married couples who have come through difficult times and rebuilt a happier life together.

Some of the topics covered:-

- preparation for marriage or remarriage
- keeping warmth alive
- reappraisal of expectations and commitments
- giving a partner space whilst preserving togetherness
- building better communications
- grandparent problems: from both sides of the fence
- facing hardships, regrets, jealousy, moods, sexual problems, life alone after a break up, and step children's hostility.

★ ★ ★

Hassle or Harmony
Every PARENT'S Choice
by
Hroth and Victor Bennett

ELM PUBLICATIONS

First published in 1987 by Elm Publications,
Seaton House Kings Ripton, Cambs PE17 2NJ
Printed and bound by Billings & Son Ltd.,
Worcester.

 British Library Cataloguing in Publication Data

Bennett, Hroth
    Hassle or harmony : every parent's choice
    1. Family 2. Interpersonal relations
    I. Title II. Bennett, Victor
    306.8'7   HQ734

    ISBN 0-946139-65-2

BSD CS7

CONTENTS

THE AUTHORS

Hrothgaarde Bennett, M.A., (Cantab) was a Senior Lecturer in Child Psychology and a family therapist over many years. Her lifetime of practical experience in this field has especially fitted her to pick out the vital skills a parent needs to learn and use when bringing up a family.

Hroth later developed a technique of audio-tape counselling for parents and their children of all ages. Through this medium she was able to make contact with and help many ordinary families struggling with temporary hassle as well as others with more serious and long lasting problems.

Vic Bennett, O.B.E., BSc., F.I.E.E., is a chartered engineer whose contribution is based on practical experience culminating in close contact with 13 grandchildren. He became enthusiastically convinced that the PRACTICAL APPROACH described in this book can be followed with advantage by ANYONE seeking greater understanding between the generations.

Being a down to earth engineer he did not, at first, have much time for what he described as complicated psychological ideas on child rearing. He trusted his 'no nonsense' approach which he felt came naturally to any caring parent. Later he changed his mind. "I have to admit I was sadly mistaken. My way landed me in a lot of unnecessary hassle! I then found that the approach I had scorned worked wonders not only for me but for many other families who I saw transformed into happier more companionable people in a comparatively short time. My scepticism soon changed to enthusiasm and I felt a strong urge to pass on the information to others. Hence my involvement in writing this book with the layman's point of view and difficulties in mind."

ACKNOWLEDGMENTS

Special thanks to members of our own family for their help and support in putting the book together. We feel privileged in our remarkably warm friendship with all our thirteen grandchildren who supplied many vivid examples of how children feel and react.

We would also like to thank all those people who read the manuscript and who made helpful suggestions. We are very grateful to the parents and youngsters who allowed us to use verbatim conversations and transcripts from counselling audio-tapes. Names, of course, have been changed and please, throughout the book, read he/she where for convenience only *he* or *she* alone has been used in the text.

FOREWORD

There are families whose lives are all sunshine and laughter . . . but most of us face days of frustration over apparent trivialities that escalate out of all proportion.

No parent decides to nag or put their child down deliberately. Even with the best of intentions words slip out that start up bickering and cause irritation. We want our children to be polite, not rude; to be enthusiastic, not lazy; to be caring and cooperative, not selfish and contrary; but we do not always get what we want.

This book is intended to help you to improve the quality of your family relationships. We were urged to write it by parents who had benefited from learning the new skills described and who, by using them appropriately and selectively, had soon seen positive results.

This book is for ALL FAMILIES at ALL STAGES and is not just for those with problems. Through its different approach to DISCIPLINE, GOOD COMMUNICATION and WAYS TO RESOLVE CONFLICTING INTERESTS AND VALUES it leads parents and children towards greater mutual sensitivity and understanding. This tends to prevent hassle while encouraging an atmosphere of MUTUAL RESPECT and WARMTH.

For families who face stressful relationship problems, the book suggests ways to find practical solutions.

We believe that a happy family life is beyond price. We KNOW that the approach we have described can go a long way towards achieving just such a life.

CHAPTER 1 : Is Constant Family Hassle Inevitable?

Take an ordinary day in the life of any family; it may begin with everyone having a grumble, starting from nothing in particular:

MOTHER: "The alarm went off half an hour ago; do hurry, you'll be late for school. Daddy can't wait for you."

BRUCE: "Oh stop nagging, Mum." Dad then has his little crack:

DAD: "The coffee isn't exactly hot this morning."

MOTHER: "Well heat it up. I can't do six things at once."

DAD: "Six? Two seems to be your limit!"

BRUCE: "Gosh! Look! Wendy has mucked up my homework."

WENDY: "That isn't fair. Why always blame me?"

MOTHER: "Bruce, don't hang about or you will have to walk."

DAD: "Well, I'm off. Have a pleasant day, darling."

MOTHER: "Some hope! I wish I could walk out and leave all this mess. Now why is Peter yelling?"

WENDY: "I thumped him. He tore off a piece of Bruce's homework. It wasn't me, you've all got it in for me."

So the day gets off to a start with friction and discontent in the air. The end of the day may be even less peaceful. Dad may come home wanting to relax and be cosseted; Mum may be bored and want to go out for a change; the kids want attention and to tell of their day's adventures. Everyone wants to look at different TV programmes. No one gets to do what they want to do when they want to do it.

The very structure of a family makes it prone to friction. A group of people differing in age and sex is thrown together for a large proportion of their time. Each has his or her wishes, feelings, tastes and values, many of which are likely to conflict with those in the rest of the family. Such a situation is bound to generate problems that need phenomenal patience and wisdom in order to prevent permanent hassle. As few possess these qualities, it is not surprising that many negative feelings are aroused. These include irritation, hurt, anger, worry, frustration and jealousy. All these feelings produce TENSION. This is the state where people feel tense, het up and on edge.

The trouble with tension is that it is self-generating. For example, angry words are met by angry responses which in turn provoke more anger and so on until those involved are furious. When this happens the spirit of cooperation is lost, people fall into combatative win-or-lose situations, tempers flare and a spiral of ever rising tension is built up.

Tension Building Doubts and Anxieties

In addition to these conflicts of needs and wishes for both parents and children, there is a steady stream of tension building doubts that chip away at peace of mind. Mum wonders: "Should I feed the baby when he cries? Should I pick him up or should I let him scream? Would a good slap solve the problem or would it just make things worse? Should I spend time with the kids or

1

talk to Dad? I'll miss my favourite TV programme anyway. Should I, for the sake of peace, let Dad off his share of the domestic load? Should I speak to Mandy about her late hours and unsuitable boy friends or am I being unreasonable? Will talking to her about the Pill just encourage her to have sex? There is always so much to harass me and I am always so busy. I'm certainly not the carefree girl I was. I wonder if Bill is getting bored and wanting a change? Is there someone else he fancies?"

Dad may be wondering if he should be more firm with the kids when they are disobedient. Would a stricter attitude spoil a nice easy relationship? Is it a wife's job to look after the kids and see them to bed? Should he help or would this be the thin end of the wedge? Should he talk to Mark about how messy he looks? But what if Mark told him to mind his own business? How should he get back to a closer relationship with Mark, who now seems to confide only in his friends? And what about his wife? Are things all right there? He and Carol seem to be getting on each other's nerves and flying off the handle a lot more easily than in the early days. The list of questions may differ, but it is always a long one.

Children, too, are beset with anxieties: "Mum and Dad always seem so busy with grown-up things, they don't seem to care enough about me. They just nag and order me about; they don't seem to care how I feel. They don't really understand; if they loved me they would give me more of what I want. Why do they ask me to behave in a way that makes me seem odd to my friends? Can't they see that things have changed? There is no doubt that Mum and Dad make me feel bad when I fail to live up to their standards. I'm sure Mum loves Julia more than me; that's not fair. They make me feel so useless sometimes. Life is so complicated; they never explain the really tricky things."

These kinds of anxieties make for discontent. Parents know it is necessary to understand and help the young with their problems. Yet they dare not be too inquisitive or appear to pry. How difficult it is to know how much to warn, how much to leave unsaid and what to explain openly.

These worries can only increase with all the rapid change, the transience of standards and values, economic and mass-media pressures. Sometimes it is tempting to give up, do nothing and let life take its course. Sadly, if this is done, the problems do not just go away; they tend to multiply, until they could easily destroy the unity of the family, and the dream of a secure and happy home begins to fade.

Harmony Is Possible

By and large, the outlook for the modern family appears fairly bleak. Yet some do manage to overcome many of these difficulties and create an atmosphere of harmony. The following comments made by a few of the youngsters at a teenager's discussion group show this is possible:

"My Mum often knows how I feel without my having to explain. I know she was young once, but for all that, times have changed a lot and I'm surprised when she gets it right so often."

"My home is all right. I wouldn't swap it for anything."

"If anyone gets up against my brother or sister, they'll have to deal with me first. Our family sticks together and that goes for our parents too."

"There are plenty of arguments, but in the end things work out pretty well. We agree to give and take and everyone tries to see the other's point of view."

"I like to take my friends home because they are always welcome."

"My old man isn't such a bad old stick; in a dust up, I can count on him. In fact he sometimes quite surprises me!"

"I can count on my parents completely. They may tell me off but I know they will never let me down, even if I get into trouble."

The parents of the children who made these comments would have enjoyed being flies on the wall during their discussion. All of us want a happy, loyal family and a secure home. Most of us put our hearts into achieving this end. Some manage to succeed and everyone would like the key to their success. It is certainly not dependent on money. The many unhappy rich families and happy poor ones are proof of this. Nor is it a question of luck or class, of colour, creed or status. Nor does endless self-sacrifice seem to be the answer; in the long run it so often leads to a feeling of having missed out and of not being appreciated. A housebound mother expressed her reaction in this way, "I gave up my job to look after the family and where has it got me? The kids take little notice of me and certainly show no appreciation of what I have done for them. In fact I feel little more than part of the furniture and I really regret the step I took". Her discontent festered in spite of meaning to do the best for her family. We are still left with the question "What is it that makes the difference between having a happy family unit and a disgruntled one?"

The Key To Cutting Down Conflict

Fortunately, there is much that can be done to make sure that there is more harmony than hassle. First, there must be faith by both parents that not only can their marriage be made to work but that communication with their children can be kept open and easy.

Secondly, parents need to realise that the harmony will not just happen by hoping, wishing and holding high ideals. It has to be worked on in a practical way. Getting on as a family is a complex business and requires a great deal of learning as well as effort. It also calls for some knowledge of how children, as well as one's spouse, think, feel, react and behave.

The third and probably the most important step of all, is to recognise the problems, strip them of all non-essentials and then set out to tackle them. Each family's areas of conflict will be different, most will have conflicts of legitimate needs such as preferences, tastes, work or school priorities, talents or hobbies. Some will have conflicts of values. Change today is so rapid that it takes one's breath away. It is of little wonder that children's values may be poles apart from those of their parents. Hairstyles, speech, morals, politics, patriotism, and religion are all potent areas of friction between the generations. The important thing is to pinpoint the trouble spots when they appear so they can be dealt with at once. It is cheering to know that some of these problems are likely to be transitory.

Fourth, no one person, let alone a generation, can claim that their needs are paramount or their values are the correct ones. Right or wrong largely depends on which side of the fence a person sits. So understanding, not condemnation, is one of the keys of peaceful co-existence.

One thing certainly stands out from all this; conflicts within a family are inevitable. They are a fact of life that has to be squarely faced up to and dealt with. How best can this be done?

Solutions In A Nutshell

Problems can be faced with more confidence when there is a feeling of satisfaction with life and self-respect is high, so an obvious step towards family harmony lies in each member doing all they can to create these conditions in the home. Parents can do this by **building up** each other's self-image and providing the **love, encouragement and fun** that children need in order to feel secure and contented. Children can help by learning the value of listening to parents and appreciating that adults, too, have needs and wishes that deserve attention.

All this will be a help, but not a cure. Conflicts will still occur and tension build up. So it is necessary to be able to **recognise the signs of mounting tension** and develop the means to **release** it in harmless ways.

Once self-confidence runs high and tension is released, the **spirit of co-operation** will be at an optimum. Then is the time to seek **compromise solutions** acceptable to all and, in this way, allow a general feeling of understanding to predominate.

It all sounds so simple. Most real solutions are but they are so much hot air unless coupled with the secret of HOW it can be done. Otherwise it is rather like saying that, if everyone could be unselfish and forgiving, all the world's problems would be solved! Possibly true, but the question of how to achieve this dream remains unanswered.

Fortunately, the "HOWS" to minimise conflict in the family are there to be learned. This is not an impossible dream but a reality within everyone's grasp. This book deals with the "HOWS" relating to parents and their children. It tries to show:

HOW a child's self-esteem can be built up.

HOW feelings of discontent can be prevented.

HOW dissatisfied feelings can be recognised and understood.

HOW tension can be kept down and released when it runs high.

HOW to get children to listen and respond.

HOW communication with the young can be kept open.

4

HOW to find acceptable solutions to conflict with and between children. HOW, finally, when we know what to do, what further we can do to ensure that we do it, day in and day out, in a busy life, even in the face of setbacks, discouragement or plain forgetfulness!

This sets us definite targets to aim at. It is human to wonder how long it will be before we can hope to see any change. The answer is that it certainly will not be for ever and a day! It is rather like asking how long it will take to learn to drive. So much depends on our keenness, our application and how open our minds are to new ideas. A lot of "ifs" but, in spite of this, in our experience in working with parents, many families notice some change for the better in three months and see a substantial improvement in six. Where there are no specific problems then parents find that ordinary everyday family hassle is lessened within a few weeks.

The Wider Issues

Quite apart from the personal crisis of mounting stress most of us face, there is a larger problem right on our doorstep. We face child abuse, gang violence, football hooliganism and teacher baiting, let alone juvenile rape, arson, theft and murder. All of these are brought right under our noses on our TV screens. In self defense we are becoming less sensitive to violence in general but this does not mean it is any less of a menace.

We look around for someone to blame; police? government? schools?. Little do we realise that perhaps we as parents hold the answer. We are the educators who, in the end, have the greatest influence on our children. We can influence the future adult generation in becoming caring and understanding people who will be ready to accept compromises towards solutions that will benefit everyone.

Many parents today are the products of the post war years. They enjoy the new freedom from strict Victorian attitudes. They were brought up to value themselves, to fight for their rights and comforts, with countless opportunities to do as they pleased. This was a necessary stage but, in many instances, it has been at the expense of a failure to instil in present day youngsters the importance of self-discipline, and caring about others above their own immediate needs and wishes. Right now, if we want a society fit for our grandchildren, it is up to us as parents to redress the imbalance and to concentrate on teaching our children social values from infancy.

This book has been written to show a different approach to these challenging tasks. It presents two definite goals. First, it is in our own interest to create a happier, more satisfying and peaceful family life and, second, it is in the interest of society to rear children who are more caring and who know the meaning of self-discipline instead of merely fighting for their own selfish ends. On both counts our peace of mind is at stake.

(In a companion volume – *Hassle or Harmony? – Every Couple's Choice* the question of minimising the hassle between parents and the effect of a lack of parental harmony on children is discussed.)

PART I CREATING A CLIMATE FOR CONTENTMENT

CHAPTER 2: Keeping Fit Emotionally

Why is it that some families seem able to keep tension down to a minimum? Are they just lucky or has life, by chance, dealt them less than their fair share of trouble? In fact, neither suggestion is true. Their success lies in their ability to handle trouble when it arises. The clue to this ability lies in Emotional Health, which is something each one of us needs to make sure our family enjoys.

The Basic Emotional Needs

Emotionally-fit people feel content; their self-respect is high and their self-confidence is such that they are prepared to cooperate without feeling insecure and at risk. Those suffering from emotional malnutrition feel the opposite and are for ever on the defensive.

Most people recognise the advantage of keeping physically fit; few even consider the implications of being emotionally fit. Yet just as we need food and exercise to keep in good physical shape, so we need emotional "food" if we are to maintain emotional well-being.

What then is this emotional food that we all need and where does it come from? Its most usual source is from those around us. Members of our own family can be the chief providers. Emotional needs are varied and complex but can be grouped under these headings:

1) *To feel loved and wanted come what may*

This entails a sense of belonging and being loved for oneself unconditionally. It brings the sense of security that comes with the confidence that nothing can destroy this love. Children should never lack this vital food.

2) *To feel successful*

This is a state where self-esteem runs high. It carries with it a sense that success will follow any effort made and with it comes the self-confidence to face responsibilities and to achieve expectations. It is the exact opposite to: "I am a failure", "I am useless", "I will never achieve what I want".

3) *To have fun in living*

This means experiencing the pleasures that come through the senses and enjoying the carefree fun that sugars the bitter pill of boredom and frustration. It also means living with a sense of sparkle and *joie de vivre*. For children it can be expressed in carefree playing, such as splashing through muddy pools without being told not to dirty their clothes. The surest signs of fun in living are spontaneous laughter and smiling faces.

These basic emotional needs are what we all require to keep emotionally fit and so to feel in harmony with our surroundings and ready to co-operate with those around us. Unfortunately, these needs so often remain unfulfilled, and deprivation of any or all of them results in emotional malnutrition. The effects of this can be both serious and long lasting.

The Unrecognised Complaint – Emotional Hunger

Parents want their children to be happy, healthy and successful people. This is especially true nowadays when families are usually planned and the advent of a child is a welcome and exciting prospect. So, a great deal of goodwill should exist. There is likely to be a built-in readiness on the part of parents to make some sacrifices in their lifestyle to meet the needs of their children. Few realise how great these sacrifices will have to be and for how long they will have to continue.

With the stage set so fair it is not surprising that parents show pride and joy when the baby arrives. They make sure their child is warm and comfortably dressed, has a smart pram and cot, and that he is well fed. His mental development is carefully monitored; each step forward is a call for rejoicing. With all the physical needs so well catered for, it is significant that the emotional needs are so often neglected. It can only be assumed either that there is no realisation of the need or that its importance is underrated.

Why is this so? Many of the books and magazines on child rearing that find their way into the home give ample space and emphasis to the physical and mental needs of the child. They go into great detail on the routine to be followed to ensure comfort, health and satisfactory mental progress. These are the tangible unknowns that a mother feels are necessary to study and seek advice over. Even when a book does lay some stress on emotional needs, parents often tend to dismiss the warnings with a casual glance and little follow-up. This can be a sad neglect with serious consequences.

To further aggravate the situation there is a commonly held belief that if a child is born mentally sound, there is no special need to do anything to keep him that way. The belief is that a child's emotional development will take care of itself and that, if he does show any of the emotional oddities such as exaggerated aggressiveness, withdrawal or even super goodness, then these are just a chance of birth, like blue eyes or curly hair. The result is that neglect in the emotional field is more commonplace than it should be.

It also appears that not only is the need for emotional nutrition insufficiently appreciated but, even when the symptoms of this type of malnutrition appear and shout for attention, they are often ignored. Repeated misbehaviour, in contrast to healthy mischief, is one of these symptoms.

Any doctor, called out at 2 a.m. by an over anxious mother for a triviality, will vouch for parental concern over physical ills. Analogous examples of concern over emotional ailments cannot be quoted for the simple reason that there are none. How many parents have sought professional advice when a child has constant nightmares, is afraid of the dark, refuses to leave mother's side or refuses to get into his bath? All these are symptoms, just as are vomiting, a headache, a runny tummy or a boil. The important difference is that the causes of these physical symptoms are usually short-lived and often cure themselves, while emotional upsets are reinforced by neglect and can become long-term, hard to cure, deep-rooted complaints.

A mother might be unhappy, even ashamed, to show her child to her neighbours or friends if he is thin, pale, spotty or yelling with stomach-ache. Yet the same mother will display with pride a fat pink cherub, beautifully dressed, clinging to her skirts, refusing to be left alone for a second and showing all the signs of a serious lack of confidence. "She is so shy", mother may say with a loving smile. Her child is in fact asking for help, but the urgency of the plea goes unnoticed.

The Effects Of Emotional Malnutrition

If a mother fails to feed her child she is filled with remorse, even though the missed meal may have done little or no harm. However, if she fails to meet his need for love, she may brush this aside as of little consequence, even though the harm could be considerable. The same principle applies if a parent misses those vital opportunities to recognise a child's first success, or by constant nagging kills a child's sense of fun.

So what are the effects of emotional hunger? The first signs are seen in a child's moods and in the feelings he expresses. He may become aimless and dispirited, fearful of new people or new situations. On the other hand, he may become demanding, grabbing all he can for himself, regardless of others. The one common factor is discontent with life. As the deprivation continues, stronger and more negative feelings arise, including anger, resentment, hurt and fear. These feelings in turn trigger off many different types of misbehaviour.

When such behaviour is rebellious or annoying it is noticed and should ring the "emotional hunger" alarm bell. However, if the child quietly withdraws into himself and gives the appearance of being a quiet, shy, somewhat unapproachable person, then he stirs up no friction and, although his symptoms are just as serious, they are liable to be overlooked. In fact these nonsense free symptoms may point to a deep unhappiness and are just as urgent a distress signal as those of a child who continually bites, screams or lies. Both children are showing the signs of emotional problems and the family should be alive to the warning that something is wrong.

Adults readily recognise the effects of emotional deprivation in themselves. We all know the discontent and depression that come with feeling unwanted, unsuccessful or bored. It should, then, be easy to recognise similar feelings in children. There is, however, a possible complication. Children may not consciously hide their feelings, but they may well disguise them if they arouse a sense of insecurity or guilt. For example, a child who feels a lack of confidence in himself may react to someone who is weaker in a bullying, aggressive way, thereby trying to deceive both himself and others as to the true state of his feelings.

When symptoms of emotional upset appear in children this is a clear message, saying "I feel hungry for love. I feel hurt, angry, bored. I don't know what to do."

It is a cry for help or, at least, a warning of rising tension which should not be ignored.

Behind Every Symptom Lies A Cause

It is important to remember that persistent misbehaviour is a SYMP-TOM, a sign that something is wrong. The CAUSE often lies deeper and can be related to emotional malnutrition — that is to some unsatisfied emotional need.

The physical analogy should help to make this clear. A stomach-ache is a symptom. The cause may be anything from simple indigestion, to an ulcer, appendicitis, food-poisoning or even cancer. The symptom merely sounds the alarm, and proper diagnosis must follow to track down the cause before treatment can be attempted.

Unfortunately, in both physical and emotional problems, there is not always a straightforward direct link between symptom and cause. There is often a third factor, a sort of trigger, that lies between the two. Consider appendicitis. Here it is a foreign body lodging in the appendix that triggers the inflammation which results in the warning symptom of pain. In the case of a peptic ulcer, worry can trigger the conditions that cause the formation of an ulcer, which in turn announces its presence by the symptom of pain.

The emotional pattern follows similar lines. If a child is deprived of any of its emotional needs this can, as we have seen, trigger feelings such as anger, hurt, frustration or fear. These feelings then find expression in the symptom of misbehaviour. Clearly it is of no use trying to deal with the problem by treating the symptom, which in this case is the misbehaviour. Yet, so often, this is exactly what parents do. They react to behaviour without a thought for what caused it. For example:

"You naughty boy! Fancy breaking your best toy."

"Stop snivelling. You'll drive me mad."

"Don't look so pathetic. Let go of my dress."

The chain of events should now be clear. Hunger for love, self-esteem or fun can cause negative feelings. These in turn can lead a child to behave in an unsatisfactory and uncooperative way. It follows that the root cause must be tackled. This is the emotional hunger, not just the misbehaviour.

This chapter has probably introduced some new and perplexing ideas. Parents may have felt they were doing everything they had been advised to do and now they are told seemingly harmless behaviour may be a warning of emotional hunger in their child, and any lapse in their own reactions may do harm. Don't despair! A child is a tough little creature and it takes quite a lot of mistakes to produce any lasting ill-effects.

First, if you are reading this book to know more about rearing a happy family, please realise none of us is perfect, no child or family is perfect, and it is learning by mistakes and learning from our children, as well as keeping our minds open to new ideas, that will help us to succeed.

Secondly, take heart, do not expect to change ingrained habits overnight. It takes a while to change even one's simple reaction to unwelcome behaviour from "What do *I* feel about this?" to "What is causing this?" So every time you know you have avoided some hassle by giving the right emotional food give yourself a pat on the back and know you are going in the right direction.

As prevention is always better than cure, the best way is to ensure that the child's emotional needs are fully met. In this way the negative trouble-making feelings are kept to a minimum. How this is achieved will be dealt with next.

CHAPTER 3: Meeting The Need For Love And Affection

We All Need To Feel Loved

The emotional needs of people are many and varied but pride of place goes to those falling under the heading of feeling loved and wanted. Being starved of love really hurts! High in any child's priorities is the feeling:

"I want to be loved whether I am good or bad."

"I want to be loved just because I am me."

This need for love starts from babyhood, continues throughout childhood, persists in adulthood and is as strong as ever with the onset of old age. For children it is as important as being fed and clothed.

How The Need Is Recognised

Children's questions, especially if repeated, can give a clue to their anxieties in this direction. They may ask:

"Will you love me when I grow up?"

"Do you still love me even when I am naughty?"

"Will you miss me when I am at school?"

"Will you love me when I am dead?"

"Will you love me as much as the new baby?"

Even if a child does not voice his concern over being loved 'come what may', it is more than likely that the concern is there. Every child seeks reassurance that he is loved, and yearns for the feeling of safety that follows such reassurance. He wants to be sure that he has a special place in the family, that he matters for himself and that he has a valued part to play. A child will be more co-operative and reasonable when so reassured. So many small events in daily life tend to raise his doubts. The following examples include some of the careless remarks made by parents to others in front of their children, which even when said jokingly, are often taken seriously:

"Kids are an absolute menace. They are more trouble than they are worth."

"It would be such fun dressing a girl. Boys are so dull."

"Being with children all day is enough to send one round the bend."

There are many other things that chip away at a child's confidence and cause "Am I loved?' anxieties: for example, excessive attention to a new baby, unconscious favouritism towards one child, and remarks that suggest rejection, such as:

"You are driving me mad. I wish you would get lost for a bit."

"Why can't you be more like Bill? He is such a helpful boy."

The simple act of loving is not enough; it must be expressed constantly and in a form to which the child will respond. This is especially true when reassurance is called for. Parents should never grow complacent but keep up an obvious demonstration of love and should show that it is still there in moments of anger and stress. Complacency needs to be watched for as it can so easily creep in undetected.

1) *By body language*

As parents we have to show love positively and convincingly. Children never take our love for granted, so it needs to be shown continually, even if a child is undemanding of it. This is especially true of teenagers. By paying attention to a child even at inconvenient times, one can make him feel special and valuable in his own right. Presents and treats are no substitute for showing love.

It is essential to use the body language of love. The soft touch, quick squeeze or hug, kissing and some physical contact are necessary for children of all ages and nearly all the time!

Girls need this reassurance, especially from father, just before they reach their teens and after. It helps them to feel pleasantly feminine and so lessens their need to seek out this reassurance from boys, who give it only too willingly! Fathers often suddenly drop demonstrative affection when their daughter reaches 11 to 12 years of age. They say it embarrasses. It might help them to overcome this if they realised the possible consequences of not making her feel loved and appreciated as a girl. If a girl is confident that she is attractive as a woman she is far better able to withstand the pressures of her peers, which might tempt her away from the values and ideals she has gradually absorbed from her family and now holds as her own.

Love is most easily conveyed by the eyes. Looking directly at a child should not be limited to special times of praising or rebuking. The eyes should be used to convey a continuous unique deep contact which says, "I am in touch with you: I care about you". People in love never tire of looking at each other.

Some children may begin to withdraw and avoid eye contact and physical closeness. When this happens it is no use feeling rebuffed and retaliating in kind, or trying to force a warmer response. Instead, especially suitable times have to be chosen to show demonstrative love when the child's need for being cared for is at its height. This occurs when they are ill, when sharing jokes or interests, when in trouble at school or when they have done something to be proud of. In these circumstances overt love is more likely to be accepted.

Sometimes this withdrawal may be coupled with signs of fear, hurt or resentment. Then it is a message saying damage has been done and something in the relationship needs to be mended. Withdrawal can also be a test, saying, "I want to see if you retaliate or show that you love me even when I don't respond".

2) *By use of words*

For the most part love is expressed by words. Terms of affection, pet names, phrases showing agreement, reassurance, understanding, approval or sympathy, can all come into play. Such expressions as:

"I love you because you are you."

"I still love you even when you annoy me."

"I love you, come what may."

These phrases may sound a bit forced at first, but if spoken with sincerity they will reflect exactly what the child wants to hear. It is worth stressing that "loving come what may" in no way implies "always liking what you do", nor does it mean agreeing with whatever may be done or said. It does, however, set a climate of togetherness, building up a relationship that is positive, supportive and secure and so helps allay a child's lurking doubts and fears.

Teenagers too, always retain some measure of the younger child's need for verbalised reassurance. This need is seldom admitted by the older child, but it is nontheless welcome when it is met. Simple phrases such as the following are music to their ears:

"That's fine."
"You look great."
"I like the way you tackled that."
"I don't know what I would do without you."
"How very thoughtful of you!"

It is essential that these words of affection and approval do not come out of thin air and so sound hollow, but are made in response to some specific action or occasion. They should be made as genuinely thoughtful comments at the right moment. But it is failing to say them when they should be said that really hurts a child.

3) *By showing a child he is wanted and needed*

Being made to feel a unique person, although an integral part of a group, is not the contradiction that it may sound. Family times for doing things together should be made as happy as possible. This applies especially to meal times and to doing chores, and even to watching TV. Everyone can be given a chance to contribute and, when opportunity presents, made to feel that they have an individual part to play. Conversation can be directed to include everyone and comments sought, not only collectively but individually too. Making sure that everyone contributes may seem obvious, but in a family where one child talks less, or is slow to express an opinion, it is easy to overlook their lack of participation. A remark like "I would like to hear what Angus thinks" immediately makes Angus feel his opinion matters.

Picking out an individual for a special job also makes him think he matters and is needed. Sometimes love is denied by overlooking an individual, by showing preferences for another and giving unfair privileges. These privileges are easy to give to the oldest and the youngest in the family. The ones in the middle, however, often tend to suffer from lack of identity, and special care is needed to rectify this. It may be possible to stress some aptitude and grant a privilege around that. For example, "Joanna is so clever at arranging flowers, I vote we leave her to put them where she thinks best". When parents begin to hear such comments as "It's always Sean who gets his way", or "Rod is the oldest so he gets all the fun", or "Boys get away with anything", then it is time to take notice. These are clear warnings that all is not well and that the children feel that love is not being shared out equally.

Fun together as a family is important but the need of a child to relate personally to mother and father is more important. Children treasure opportunities of being alone with a parent, especially in larger families. So a short time should be allocated to each youngster, and however busy the parent, this 'Time Alone' should not be missed unless it is quite unavoidable.

Many parents think they are doing a favour by inviting one of their child's friends to join them on an outing. If this is particularly requested by the child, then well and good, but if the initiative has come from the parent and is only a thinly disguised excuse to be able to be free to chatter to an adult friend, it will not be appreciated. The child may decide correctly that Mum or Dad finds being alone with him too much of an effort. The privilege of an outing alone with a parent will go a long way towards making a child feel he is a worthwhile companion and that he is loved for himself.

"Come on Bill, let's go for a walk. Just you and me."

"Let's go shopping together, Ruth. You'll be such a help choosing something that really suits me."

It is so little to give and yet brings so much appreciation.

Young children especially, get a happy, secure feeling of belonging when sharing jobs with their parents, even if the help is only token. They love to copy Mum and Dad, and later the situation might change to Mum and Dad helping out with things initiated by their child.

4)   *By writing notes and letters*

Another little used but most effective way of making a child feel loved lies in the writing of little notes that come as a heart-warming surprise. The value of letters during a long separation is obvious. Not so obvious, but just as valuable, is the little note during short periods apart. Imagine the joy of a daughter opening her lunch-box at school to find a note from her Mum, "Have put in some of your 'specials', darling. Hope you enjoy them. Have a fun day. Love, Mum"; or a son returning from school and finding a note from Dad, "Hi Mark! — Hope the day went well. Longing to hear all about the rugger match when I get home. Have one or two problems I'd like to talk over with you. Any chance of a chat? Cheers, Dad"; or perhaps left by a bedside, "Bless you dear for being so helpful today with all the big crowd here. I know you had lots of your own things to do which got shelved. Happy dreams — Mum".

The fact that these notes are so personal and for his or her eyes only, makes them especially pleasant and welcome. They are like a blazing sign that reads : "Someone really cares about me". Finally, fathers need to make a special effort in this direction. Dad is the one, because of his work, who is usually away from home the most and so has least contact with his children on an 'alone' basis. His notes and letters are, for this reason, greatly appreciated.

5) *By avoiding rebuke in times of stress*

When something disagreeable happens, like torn clothing or a precious glass broken and it is the child's fault, parents tend to give vent to their natural feelings in the following ways:

"You silly child! Look what you have done!"

"How stupid and careless of you!"

"'How clumsy can you get!"

"Oh, what a mess! I could murder you!"

This sort of reaction, while normal enough, only adds to the catastrophe. Controlling this sort of outburst is difficult but nonetheless necessary. Scathing criticism, at a moment of stress for the child, bites deep and harms the relationship. The child longs to hear reassurance such as, "Hard luck", or "Tough", or even "Mummy is a bit upset but it was an accident".

No amount of expressed annoyance wlll repair the damage, but by using the right words or even by saying nothing and giving a comforting squeeze of the shoulder, some good can come out of disaster. Relationships, after all, are more important than stained carpets or broken treasures. If a child feels a sense of love in adversity his response will be both positive and powerful.

How The Need Should NOT Be Met

Some ways of showing love are positively harmful. Love can be too possessive; it can smother and seem to bind, as reflected by this child's reaction:

"Sometimes I feel I want to push my mother away and stop her holding on to me. She says I can do what I want but in the same breath she makes out that she loves me so much that she wants me around all the time and resents my making friends."

Single parents can, in the same way, make excessive demands and play on their loneliness as a means of binding a child to their side. Love can also be used to satisfy a parent's longing to live through their child's life. This puts a great strain on the child when success is involved:

"My dad will collapse if I fail my 'A's. He never went to university and is set on my doing so. His life seems to revolve around my career."

The need to love should not be taken as a need to spoil a child. Real harm can often result from giving in to unreasonable demands. Problems can be increased if this is done and it leads to resentment and temper tantrums when eventually the child fails to get his way. Showing love should be coupled with showing clear displeasure at any unsatisfactory action and there should be no hesitation in denying a request when the occasion demands.

The same applies when a child whines on and on for a sweet or something else he wants. Even though nearly driven to distraction it is FATAL for a mother to give in even ONCE. A firm "Not now", repeated without rancour, as often as necessary, needs to be said. A child soon learns whether his mother can be worn down to give way. This is a battle that is worth winning once and for all.

Love can be over-effusive. It then loses its value if not backed up with equal concern and unselfishness:

"My mum's quick enough to say that she loves me but jolly slow when it comes to taking time off to listen to me."

The showing of love between a father and daughter or mother and son can easily begin to show an element of veiled seductiveness that has mildly sexual undertones. For example, a father might leer at his daughter and exclaim, "My, you look good enough to eat tonight. I wish I was taking you out".

This tendency needs to be recognised as soon as it begins to creep in and is naturally better avoided. However light or joking the approach, it can leave children with a feeling of distaste that could colour their attitude to sexual relationships later. Sometimes the children themselves may initiate the process. This needs to be nipped in the bud and not encouraged or played up to. Incestuous relationships are much more common than people expect and noticing signs of something which seems out of place may save a lot of trouble later.

Sincere love means many things to many people, but to everyone it means being special in someone's eyes. Hunger for love, rivalry and feeling rejected are hard enough for adults to bear, but for children they are catastrophic. When a child feels unloved he often turns to loving himself and himself alone. If there is no one to please but himself he soon develops into the perfect egoist and, in the end, becomes other people's as well as his own worst enemy.

When love is in plentiful supply then the natural response is to try and please, to do what the loved one wishes and to admire and copy him. This is how a child learns to comply, to absorb ideas and values from his parents who love him and who, in turn, he wishes to please and emulate.

Being loved, then, is the first ingredient towards building up a picture of oneself as a worthwhile person. In spite of being loved, some adults still do not like the picture they have of themselves. This is equally true with children. As a result they lack confidence. Their self-esteem has to be built up in other ways so that they can find the courage to face life as independent people. How parents can help this process is the subject of the next chapter.

CHAPTER 4: Building Up Self-Esteem

The Need To Feel Successful

Everyone feels more comfortable, relaxed and pleased with life if their picture of themselves is satisfactory. Most people like to feel that they are respected, capable and kind. They like to feel that they matter and are able to meet their problems with confidence and some hope of success.

No one should expect their self-image to be without blemish. There is no harm in recognising our deficiencies realistically, although for real contentment, it is necessary for the scales to come down fairly heavily on the positive side. Otherwise there may be a sense of failure, inferiority and inability to cope with life and people.

It is the same with children. Their self-image or self-esteem needs to be nurtured and fostered from early childhood if they are to cope with life with courage and determination. Children show how much they enjoy success when they say:

"I can do that!"

"I know the answer."

"Let me show you. I know how."

Not only do they enjoy success, but they want to know that their successes are recognised. They love encouragement and the opportunity to test themselves out. They also like to feel that their parents have confidence in them and believe they can succeed. Phillip, aged seven, said: "When I play at balancing on a plank, I wobble if I am told to be careful not to fall and hurt myself. I do much better when my parents believe I can do it safely". Teenager Lucy said: "My mother never shows that she has any confidence in my common sense. It doesn't help. I find I want to be sensible when people trust me but not when they nag and tell me exactly what to do and what not to do".

Recognising When Self-Esteem Is Lacking

In children, a lack of confidence may show as over-timidity or shyness. A child may not accept himself as he is. He may be afraid to make friends, fearing that no one will like him; he may want everything done for him and seek constant support from grown-ups. He may fear to do anything alone in case he fails to come up to expectations. Here are some comments made by children with poor self-esteem:

"My Dad is always expecting me to win. Even if I come second I feel a flop."

"It's awful to be a soppy girl. I wish I was a boy."

"Other children always pick quarrels with me. They don't seem to like me."

There are other children who disguise their lack of confidence. They pretend to be brave and put on a superior face to the world. They bully smaller children and choose friends whom they can dominate. They make a lot of noise and give a lot of cheek; they constantly look for praise and try to cover their lack of success with boasts, excuses and fibs. Julian was one such and he said: "If I worked harder I could easily be top of our class, but it is sissy to swot".

Building The Foundations For Self-Esteem

Every child can be helped to accept himself in terms of his total make-up and, in so accepting himself, he comes to feel unique and special. Inquisitiveness about himself needs to be encouraged. If he is a boy he should be pleased to be a boy and the same applies to a girl. Parents need to praise masculinity and femininity.

Parents who accept their children's abilities and shortcomings help their children accept them too. When there is a serious disability, then overcoming it, even to a small extent, can bring self-respect. Thalidomide children provide a wonderful example of this. No handicapped child thrives on pity and those around him have to see round the handicap to the person himself. Once this happens, a more positive attitude soon develops.

It is a mistake to think that children with special ability, or who are clever and talented, are necessarily self-confident. In many instances they feel they never come up to expectations. The goals they set themselves and the ones set by their parents and teachers are often out of their reach and consequently they feel a sense of failure.

Once a child learns to relax with himself, he will be ready to relax with others. A relaxed child is easy to recognise because he is not over-anxious and tensed-up about himself. The child who always sees himself as failing to cope with life wastes a lot of energy on unnecessary worries instead of conserving this energy to use on things that matter.

The process of building up self-esteem starts from birth. The earlier an effort is made to encourage a child to feel that, with sufficient effort, he can succeed, the better. The younger the age the easier it is to build up and reinforce the pattern of success, and this pattern is likely to be reflected throughout life.

This build-up process can be started by parents being on the alert and trying to be there when success of any kind is achieved for the first time. They then need to applaud the new-found skill. This comes naturally to parents when they are dealing with 1 to 2 year olds, but their interest tends to flag during the years of 3 and 4. This is a pity because these are crucial years when effort and success are most clearly connected in a child's mind. Encouragement during this period pays the best dividends for the future. An example of how to react, and how NOT to react, to a child's new-found skill is the following:

Jenny, aged 3, after much effort, including painful bangs on the nose, has just learned to wield the big broom just like mother. She proudly demonstrates her new ability in the crowded kitchen. Mother drops everything and intervenes. "Hey stop that! You'll break something. Careful of those cups.

Mummy has already swept here." As mother forcibly removes the broom, Jenny is left angry, deflated and frustrated. How much better if mother had said: "You are sweeping just like Mummy. Well done. Look, here is a mess to clear up in the passage. Try to sweep it all up." Removal of Jenny and the broom to the passage is then the answer and her continued valiant efforts can be noted and commented upon. The broom, soon abandoned in the passage, could be picked up by Mum with the comment that it has a special place where it belongs while she returns it to the cupboard.

If, on the other hand, mother picks up the broom and Jenny is treated to a general homily on being tidy and putting things away, then the joy of her recent success will count for nothing. There is, of course, a time and place for encouraging tidiness, but not when the child has just been through what to her is a mighty achievement. This achievement should, to her mind, outweigh the need for a boring lecture on tidiness. It is rather like being told to dry your feet properly when you have just swum the Channel!

Alternatives to dangerous and destructive behaviour often have to be found but, where possible, this should be done without restricting exploration and experiment and, most important, without criticism or interference at the 'moment of truth'. After all what would a matador feel if, at the crucial moment, the bull was suddenly whisked away?

These considerations do not only apply to young children. When a first poem is written, parents should share the thrill, but should ignore the scruffy paper, illegible writing and failure to turn up for a meal on time. This is no time for criticism. The child's wish to persevere and succeed is actively encouraged when his success is recognised. This proves to him that effort is worthwhile.

The value of this pattern of successful endeavour cannot be overemphasised. It is especially important later in tackling school work where ability to persevere, coupled with the confidence that doing so brings success, often proves more valuable than sheer intelligence.

Encouraging Self-Regulation

The earlier a child can be encouraged to make decisions for himself, the sooner his confidence will grow. This is the start of self-reliance from which a sense of responsibility will develop. A simple way to start is to present the child with suitable alternative choices and let him make up his own mind which he wants. Food is a ready-to-hand medium for this exercise. The alternatives need to be limited, but the choice, however simple, is there.

"How would you like your egg? Boiled or scrambled?"

"What would you like on your bread, jam or Marmite?"

This rather than, "Here is a Marmite sandwich". Endorsement of the choice made can also add to the child's growth of confidence.

The start of making choices can be coupled with the idea that problems can be divided into three main categories: a child's problem, a parent's problem and a family problem. A child's problems can then be clearly identified for him and he needs to be allowed to solve them for himself as soon as he is able. He will make mistakes: some will be painful and costly lessons, but what better way is there to learn and to build self-reliance?

For instance, eating is a child's problem although many mothers feel it is theirs! No healthy child will starve indefinitely if offered food. A great deal of argument can be avoided if a child is allowed from the start to choose how much he wants and is led to understand that having made the choice, he sticks to it. Deficiency in a child's diet due to fads can usually be made good by alternative foods that are acceptable to him. A child should never be forced to eat by threats because food can then become a convenient weapon to use against mother and every meal soon turns into a battle. Refusal to eat is usually short-lived when the responsibility for eating is laid firmly on the child and a valuable lesson in self-reliance is learned in the process.

Clothes provide another convenient field of choice. In younger children the choice can be limited to: "Which would you like to wear — this or that?". In older children the choice can be made wider and wider until they choose for themselves what they wear from day to day and for special occasions. The choice can, in time, be extended to the buying of clothes limited, of course, by the family purse.

Time for doing chores can also be left to choice within the limits of family convenience. Doing homework is a child's problem and his responsibility entirely. This fact should be brought home to him. He may ask for help and his plea can be met, but the final responsibility is his.

Going to sleep is also a child's problem. "Put me to sleep, Mum", is a plea best resisted at all costs as it soon can become a cord that binds mother and ties her down. The process of saying 'Good night' and settling the child down is clearly a parent's responsibility but never that of actually helping the child to fall asleep.

A child's possessions, his toys, are his problem. He will soon learn that if they are broken, then that is that; they will not be replaced. If, however, they are left lying around, it becomes a family concern and a joint solution needs to be found. Mum will not accept that she has to put them away, so the child has to find a solution that is acceptable to all. A start can be made by putting the problem squarely to the child: "Well, Bill, your toys get in everyone's way. We all fall over them and can hurt ourselves. Anyway they look untidy. What do you suggest we do about it?"

Parents may find it helpful to tabulate all the problems that belong squarely to the child, encourage him to handle them and then respect his decisions. The sooner full responsibility is laid on him the better. In this way he will begin to learn the meaning of self-regulation of at least part of his life and his self-confidence and self-esteem will grow.

Inevitably, wrong choices will be made. Parents so often feel that they should use their greater experience to save their children from making mistakes. Obviously, where health and safety are involved, there must be limits

20

on what is left to the child, but these limits need to be stretched as far as possible. Every parent has to learn to live with the inconvenience, the annoyance, and sometimes the pain of seeing their youngsters making mistakes and heading for trouble while learning by experience. This price has to be paid if the child is to grow into a responsible, self-reliant person.

A sound approach to responsibility over money is to instil in the child the idea of either/or rather than both/and. How a child spends the money he earns or is given, is his business. Whether he spends it on something stupid or saves it is up to him, but he must be helped to learn that he cannot have his cake and eat it. He must not be bailed out if he runs short as this is the road to escapism rather than self-reliance.

A chance to practice handling money, clothes, social dates, even alcohol, is essential so that the basic lessons of self-regulation are learned slowly and early mistakes made at home, where they can be put right without too much trouble.

A child needs to be left to face the consequences of his own actions, however painful it might be for the parents to stand aside and watch him suffer. Once a young person begins to believe that if in trouble someone, or even the state, will bail him out, then he will be less and less prepared to struggle to look after himself when the going gets tough. Many young people try 'dropping out' and so avoiding worldly responsibilities. The day of reckoning usually comes when they have to face life and find they are ill-equipped to do so.

Games That Help To Build Up Self-Esteem

There are many games that are fun and can be used to build up self-esteem. Parents often say that they do not know how to introduce these family games, especially if the idea has not been tried before.

Children need to have reached the age of 6 to 7 years before these games are useful. At this age any game played with Mum and Dad is fun and simple instructions on how to play are all that is necessary. The chief thing to remember is that the game must be played lightheartedly and bring enjoyment.

The game chosen should help to build self-esteem and never undermine it, even indirectly. With teenagers, for the game to catch on and be a success, it has to meet some immediate social or vocational need. The following examples illustrate the point.

Game 1 – "Sending Messages"

One way to play this game is to let children choose a particular message that they want to give their parents. The message may cover a wide range of subjects, anything from "Daddy is too bossy", "We want Dad to play with us more often" to "We want more pocket money" or "We don't like being shoved out of the way when grown-up friends visit".

The choice of message is left to the children and should not be limited by having to be sensible, kind or acceptable. The children can act out the message in charades and the parents have to guess what they are trying to put over. The acting out means that the children have to take on the roles of their parents and by doing so get insight into how grown-ups 'tick'. Discussing the message after it has been guessed gives ample opportunity for everyone's voice to be heard. Parents can build up the self-esteem of one particular child by picking out his contribution or asking his opinion. In general the game allows children the opportunity to voice opinions knowing that these will be listened to with respect.

Another way to play the game is by using paper and pencil. Each person writes messages that he/she wants a particular person to receive. Everyone picks out a paper that they have not written on themselves and proceeds to guess for whom the message is intended. So long as Mum and Dad set the pattern of sending constructive, positive messages, the game never gets out of hand but ends in discussion and teaches children to accept others' points of view or alternatively to stick up for their own.

Game 2 – "This Is My Week"

This game gives each member of the family, young or old, the chance to take certain family decisions for that particular week. The family decides which decisions to include. Choosing two favourite dishes, deciding who invites friends in and when, selecting TV programmes and fixing times for family activities are some of the many possibilities.

The week that has just passed can be discussed and the general trend of "Well done for arranging this week" can be the theme. Children playing this game learn, quite quickly, to think of others and to enjoy the comfortable feeling that follows being unselfish. It gives the parents the opportunity to build on something practical. "I like the way Jean chose so and so". Negative comment can be kept to a minimum. An unpopular choice can be discussed and pros and cons brought out.

Children of all ages enjoy feeling they are in charge. There is never any difficulty in playing the game except for Mum and Dad who have to make the effort to guide the discussion into worthwhile channels and to be sure to build up each child's self-esteem where it is most needed.

Game 3 – "Giving A Talk"

This game can be played by six year olds as a story-telling game. Everyone takes a turn at adding a bit to a story which is begun and ended by a particular child. As an extension of this game, 10 and 12 year olds enjoy telling about something they have done or seen, while teenagers may like giving a short talk on a pet subject. When the family are interested in drama or debating, the game takes off readily. Few children fail to realise the advantage of being able to gather their thoughts and express them out aloud in front of others without panic or confusion.

Any child who finds answering in class a strain will welcome practise in a friendly atmosphere. Parents may have to start off and demonstrate length, style and so on. Whatever form the game takes the individual concerned becomes the centre of attention, they feel that they are worth listening to and this in itself builds self-confidence. The opportunity for family discussion is again wide open and, depending on many diverse circumstances, can often be guided towards helping children find solutions for themselves.

All these games have endless possibilities as a trigger for useful family discussions as well as providing ways to boost self-esteem and self-confidence.

The Harm Of Reinforcing A Pattern Of Failure

Parents can reinforce failure by giving too many warnings. They may predict failure and then say "I told you so" when the worst happens. Constantly nagging at a child to try harder, indirectly dubs him lazy or hopeless. Parents, meaning to be reassuring, often dismiss a child's fears or anxieties as 'silly' or 'nothing important', instead of giving the support that is needed. This dismissive way of dealing with problems makes a child feel that others don't understand and expect him to fail.

When the pattern of failure is reinforced, children often avoid making any effort to succeed. They may well try to escape failure by cheating or trusting to luck. Some may sit back and let life happen while someone else does all the hard work. If a child is allowed to get away with this attitude or parents agree "How fortunate", "How lucky" when failure is evaded, then they reinforce the feeling that something will always turn up. "Why should I bother to try too hard, except to do what I want to do?" is the attitude with which the child surrounds himself.

When finding employment after leaving school is uncertain, it is particularly important to help a child to look for a worthwhile goal and to help him feel enthusiastic about whatever he wants to do. Encouragement to want to experiment, to take initiative, is especially important for the older teenager. If his attempts in these directions are reinforced by being welcomed, noticed and encouraged and his ideas discussed, then dropping out will not seem to be an attractive alternative to trying to succeed. As an added bonus, looking for 'kicks' in other dangerous directions is far less likely to appeal. If having no job is something that has to be faced, then if he has been suitably enthused, a teenager will not give in but will try for further training or take any opportunity that offers to satisfy his self-respect.

The Effects Of Adult Quarrels

Children take great pride in their family and anything that harms the family image hits their self-esteem. Parents constantly quarrelling does just that. Obviously, if there is a serious row, then it is better not to have children around. Feelings, however, often will not wait. The muttered "Come into the bedroom" or "Come outside" are soon recognised by children for what they are — the prelude to a row. Their anxiety at the unknown outcome may even be greater than if they were there hearing it all happen.

23

Trying to hide feelings of hostility in front of children is usually a waste of time; children easily absorb atmosphere through the skin. In any event they know all about hostile feelings and tend to fear them, but it is of little use for parents to try to pretend that they never get angry with each other. Sometimes it is a great relief to a child to see temporary annoyance or anger brought into the open and got rid of in a non-destructive and impersonal way. To a child this makes sense and brings reassurance that hot tempers are not as dangerous as he feared, when Mum and Dad can cope with them and end up smiling.

When quarrels in front of younger children cannot be avoided, a reassuring explanation needs to be given such as: "Mum and Dad feel cross at the moment, just like you do sometimes. We will soon make up and then we will feel much better". This makes the row seem much more normal and so less disturbing.

It is always better if children are not drawn into parents' rows. This can be accomplished if no attempt is ever made to make them take sides. Showering children with extra food, gifts or treats is no answer or compensation for family conflict. It may relieve the parents' guilt, but it is not the comfort that the children seek. Their fear that they are helpless to intervene or control what to them is a very menacing situation can only be relieved by constant reassurance that both Mum's and Dad's love for them remains unchanged.

Final Marriage Breakdown

However commonplace separation and divorce has become, when a family breaks up the children inevitably feel a serious blow to their self-esteem. They seem to catch some of their parents' sense of anxiety and failure. This is especially so if children are made pawns in any fight over property and custody; then a child's guilt and confusion over split loyalties can only add greatly to his general anxiety. Whatever the circumstances, every effort needs to be made to restore self-esteem.

It is unkind to leave children in the dark about a break up. Parents often deceive themselves that their children do not know what is going on, whereas in fact they probably imagine much worse possibilities than actually exist. A simple explanation such as "Sometimes Mums and Dads don't want to live together anymore, but this does not mean that either of us will stop loving you as much as ever" will give reassurance to younger children. Frank discussion, putting them fully in the picture, will often help older ones weather the storm with less anxiety.

If one parent just takes off and deserts the rest of the family, then the sure love of the remaining parent needs to be expressed clearly in order to counteract fears of total desertion. Children adapt quite quickly to upheaval and catastrophe so long as they know they are fully in the picture and will not suddenly be faced with an unknown and new menace. They are greatly reassured if there is a plan for living life under the new conditions and there is a loved and loving person with whom they can share their anxieties.

The anger and frustration that children feel at the break up need to be accepted and understood. It is desperately hard for most children to accept that their parents cannot find a better answer that will leave the family complete. Children need to be able to voice their anger and hurt, instead of adding to their resentment by having to stifle their feelings.

Verbal attacks on the parents showing how badly the child feels, need to be listened to and sympathetically reflected back to the child so that it is clear that what has been said, as well as how the child feels, is understood. "It's cruel of you to leave Daddy", needs understanding, not defending. A suitable reply might be: "I can see how sorry you feel for Dad being left on his own". Or again: "You and Mum are stupid not to make up and forgive each other so that we can all be together". No logical reason for not being able to forgive and forget will serve any purpose at this moment. The best reply is a simple reflection of what the child feels: "You feel Mum and I should be sensible enough to forget our problems?". This will lead to further conversation allowing the child to express his fears and anger. When sufficient tension has been released in this way, the move towards some acceptance on the child's part can be made.

Merely justifying one's own position does little to make unhappy children feel understood. On the other hand, reassuring them that they are still loved and that their welfare has a high priority will always be welcomed, even if at first it results in dismissal and rebuff.

Moments of stress are not the best times to give homilies on having to accept the inevitable. Expressing his own feelings freely and finding they are understood is much more likely to bring acceptance of the situation from the child, even if it comes slowly. After six months one child had worked it out for himself: "I get tired of my friends in no time. I think it's amazing my Mum and Dad stuck each other for seven years!".

It is very tempting for parents to defend themselves by saying: "I'm so sorry, but . . .it isn't my fault . . . these days lots of people get divorced . . . ". The 'buts' never convince a child who is thinking about himself and hates hearing criticism of one of his parents. The skill of showing as a loving parent that one is trying one's best to understand how low the child is feeling is dealt with in Chapter 10.

In marriage, step-children will always tend to feel insecure, and antagonistic towards a step-parent, who has a difficult role and can seldom hope to replace a divorced father or mother. Step-parents need to show that they accept this and not take it as disloyalty to themselves. At best they can become loving friends and it is usually a mistake to hope for more than this, especially if the children have access to both parents.

For children to retain high self-esteem through the period of a break up they need, more than anything else, the reassurance that their parents continue to love them and that they can love and respect their parents without restraint. So the blaming and running down of one parent by the other, however justified or strong the feeling may be, needs to be avoided. It will always do harm. The happiest outcome in a divorce is for children to retain their respect for both parents. When circumstances make this impossible, an attitude of forgiveness without recrimination may prevent hate and fear of rejection haunting them for many a long day. When a parent is still feeling deeply hurt and let down this neutrality is difficult, but in the end it will prove well worthwhile.

Rebuilding Self-Esteem

It has been pointed out that a pattern of effort leading to success, with the subsequent build up of self-confidence, should start at birth and be developed through childhood to maturity.

What happens, if for any reason a parent is faced with a child who already shows a sense of failure and inferiority? Is it then too late to do anything to help? Happily the answer is that it is never too late to try. A parent faced with this problem will have an uphill task and will probably have to start at the beginning. Step by step small successes have to be encouraged, the target always within reach without too great an effort, and the child always sensing success at the end of each stage.

There are many ways that this can be done, dependent upon the age of the child. The first step is to pick on an activity that the child enjoys and would like to succeed at. Then manoeuvre the child into taking one step that he will manage successfully after a little effort. This basic principle should be applied to as wide a range of activities as possible. Gradually the child's confidence will grow with each small success, and with perseverance, the proper pattern will be established and he may begin to tackle problems on his own and to regain the necessary self-confidence to put in the effort to succeed. Two examples may help to illustrate the technique:

A six year old boy was dispirited by the activities of a younger brother who excelled at all sports. The older boy became so discouraged that he refused to make any effort to improve. He sulked and looked unhappy. "I'm no good at anything", he said. His parents bought him his first two-wheeler bike in the hope that it would give him something that his smaller brother would not be able to manage. But, after one attempt, he fell and hurt his knee and again gave up trying. The parents then pointed out that learning to ride was difficult and must be done in stages. First, he had to get used to the bike by running with it, ringing the bell and stopping by putting on the brakes. In this he enjoyed easy success. Then an obstacle course was set up through which he had to push the bike, steering to miss everything. Eventually he succeeded. "Great! Not a thing touched", commented his parents.

The next step was for the child to mount the bike at rest and push it along with both feet while balancing for short distances; then for longer distances, bringing him more success. Confidence was growing that if he kept trying he would soon be able to ride. The same process was repeated on a gentle downhill slope together with longer periods of successful balancing. There was growing excitement! Then there was gentle turning of the pedals while Dad helped him to balance, leading at last to short, self-propelled rides. Falls had to be avoided if possible and sympathy was given if they did occur. Remarks like "Get up. You'll live!" need to be avoided. Finally he went off on his own. His skill was pointed out in front of his brother and the possibility of his teaching the younger boy how to ride at a later date casually mentioned. This boosted his success and built up his self-esteem. Most importantly, he had learnt the lesson that he could succeed if he tried. After this, he could have tackled something else, such as making a model too difficult for his brother. It would have had to be made clear that making the model was beyond his brother, as step by step, he met with success. If he read better than his brother he could have been asked to read aloud to the family, moving to more and more advanced books. There should always be a new goal within reach to strive for, but the parent should never risk failure by pushing too hard.

Here is an example involving a teenager: Wendy, aged 16, had moved around a great deal. Her parents were posted to five different places in five years. Whenever she started to make friends or adapt to a new school, they moved. She got behind with her work, became discouraged and ceased to try to make new friends.

She was an attractive girl, and her relationship with a boy while her parents were abroad ended in heartbreak for her when the boy showed a preference for someone else. When her parents returned to settle in England, they found a child who showed no confidence in herself, either socially or academically, and who had no will to take any initiative or make any effort. Her parents came to understand and accept her problem. They focussed on the one safe place for her, her home, and the one safe relationship for her, which was with her father. They began to build on these two secure props.

Wendy was sent to a day school instead of the boarding school where she had been when her parents were abroad. This meant she spent a lot of time at home and her parents were able to be on the lookout for any opportunity to start something to re-arouse her enthusiasm. At her own suggestion, she began to get her father's breakfast in the morning and this proved such a success that the whole family begged her to get their supper once a week.

Her cooking, as well as the thought and effort she put into it, brought genuine appreciation, and she soon became increasingly interested in preparing meals. Her father encouraged this glimmer of real interest and took her to various gourmet pubs in the district and encouraged her to start a collection of her favourite recipes. The excursions gave her scope for meeting people, and on one such occasion she met a woman who wanted help over catering at a ski-chalet. Wendy was at first very reluctant to accept the offer but was encouraged to do so. With a definite goal in view, Wendy's confidence blossomed

27

New relationships with boys were never pushed, but in the more relaxed atmosphere of the ski holiday she met a lot of students and so slowly became less cold, suspicious and frightened. Her parents, fingers still crossed as they watched from the sidelines, got her ready agreement to take a domestic science course, by which time she was a very different and more confident person from the timid and depressed schoolgirl they had returned to find a few years earlier.

This example may help to illustrate the point that, although circumstances are infinitely variable, the basic process of rebuilding self-esteem is the same. The gift of relaxed, self-confidence is a precious one and is an advantage to any human being. It will always remain one of the emotional needs essential for contentment.

CHAPTER 5 : Putting Fun And Sparkle Into Life

After love and self-esteem, the third basic emotional food that children need is the pleasure, coming from the senses, that makes life sweet. When this is in adequate supply we feel a sense of joy in being alive and confident that life's inevitable trials can be taken in our stride. It is the most subtle and indirect of the three emotional foods and this makes its supply less than straightforward.

In fact the fear of most parents is that, given half a chance, their children will enjoy themselves too much, probably in highly unsuitable ways! Such parents may well feel that this chapter should be directed at how to damp children down rather than make them sparkle even more. This misconception needs to be put right. Fun is so often equated with getting into mischief and causing trouble, whereas the opposite is really true. Fun destroys boredom and boredom is the state of mind that leads children into looking for 'kicks' and so becoming involved in 'way-out' activities that can lead them into serious trouble. True fun, on the other hand, leads to happiness and contentment, has no underlying viciousness and makes life feel good.

Why Do Children Get Bored?

Boredom has got nothing to do with money or lack of it. There are many children with cupboards full of expensive playthings who are still bored with their lot. This happens when their interest and initiative are not aroused. The probability is that a parent or another child is needed to act as a catalyst to give encouragement and to help stimulate the imagination. Many children are forced to spend hour upon hour alone and in the end they get bored with their own company and get up to mischief.

As research on juvenile delinquency has shown, much of today's unacceptable teenage behaviour stems from boredom. Groups of young people will always seek excitement and, if they are denied the outlet of satisfying activities, it should come as no surprise when they tend to find this outlet by defying authority, destroying property and bullying those weaker than themselves.

Boredom also arises when fun is killed at birth. This happens when there are too many 'Don'ts'. Each time a child sets out to enjoy himself he may hear one of them:

"Don't rush around so much."
"Don't make such a noise."
"Don't make such a mess."
"Don't disturb Dad and stop pestering me."
"Don't get dirty."
"Don't hurt yourself."
"Don't break anything."

Faced with too many of these, a child may just as well be trussed up in a straitjacket or told to go and hibernate! From a parent's angle these comments may seem perfectly justified and accurately reflect the conflict of interests between them and their children. These 'Don'ts', however, have a real dampening effect; they spoil fun and so encourage boredom. To avoid this, parents need to take a few moments off and share in children's fun before applying the brakes. 'Don'ts' bring a sense of oppression and encourage inactivity, whereas every opportunity needs to be taken to encourage 'Doing' and laughter. We, as parents, need to accept that mess, noise, music and busy activity are often essential parts of the fun package for children. If it is possible to have somewhere where the children can do as they like, so much the better. Young children usually manage to find their own fun without too much help from parents. Even with the minimum of material and toys, they manage to make a house under a chair, or a drum from a tin can. Mud and water are all that is needed for an exciting game, newspapers can be torn up or scribbled on and plastic containers are fine for building or fitting together. As long as Mum and Dad are around to take notice occasionally, life is always fun.

Once children start school this simple type of play is not enough. They want their efforts appreciated, a companion to play with, and their opportunities for fun extended. At this stage opportunity to find fun activity needs to be created by parents, otherwise fun has little chance to survive. "I don't know what to do" will become a whine that was never heard in babyhood. If this need in older children, to find life full and interesting, is not satisfied at home, then parents should not be surprised if their children look for their excitement elsewhere.

Ways To Promote Fun And Avoid Boredom

1) *Having a positive outlook*

Parents can make a start in the right direction by laying emphasis on the amusing and interesting aspects of life while soft-pedalling on the more pessimistic side of things. A POSITIVE, optimistic outlook needs to be encouraged. For example, an attitude of "It's wet and cold outside, let's all snuggle round the fire and enjoy it" is a happier outlook than "What a fag, we can't go out in this filthy weather". Alternatively, "Let's plan how to spend the money we've got so that we can all enjoy it", rather than "We mustn't waste money. We have so little of it".

Working parents can bring home plenty of affection to compensate for their absence: they can still put their feet up and listen, share in jokes and perhaps join in games, even for a short while if they are weary. The atmosphere in the home depends so much on the occupants. It can be so dreary if everything is taken seriously, everything carefully considered and all fun banished. It can be bright and cheerful if light-hearted laughter, optimism and spontaneity are allowed to predominate and fun is given a free rein at every opportunity.

2) *Sharing interests with children*

There is no doubt that children tend to catch their parents' interests and enthusiasms. Where these are plentiful, children are seldom hard up for something to do. When parents have few or no interests, however, then it is necessary for them to find people who have and who are willing to provide fun for their children. Schools try to do this and so do the church and social services clubs. If none of these exist nearby then other families may offer to help. It is essential in every case of this kind that parents feel concerned to introduce their children to as wide a variety of interests as possible and to find out any natural talent that can be developed into an enjoyable hobby.

"But my child never keeps at anything", said one parent. In this sort of situation parents have no alternative but to keep searching and trying out an even greater range of activities until they find one that appeals. It is important to make this extra effort. For the sake of their child they may have to conjure up in themselves some temporary enthusiasm for any slight interest or talent shown. This may entail joining in and learning too, until the child's enthusiasm has developed sufficiently for him to go it alone. In Japan many parents learn the violin so as to encourage their young. Elsewhere parents join in with such things as ballet, skating, jogging, bird watching and so on, with remarkably good results.

Another parent explained her difficulty in this way: "I'm not short on ideas but I'm just not sure how to get my child started". No matter what the art, craft, sport or collection being introduced, success will depend largely on the appeal of its initial presentation. There needs to be some freedom of choice and certainly no pressure or sense of obligation. The parent needs to be enthusiastic and the effort required by a youngster, at the start, should be kept to a minimum. It is also important to have an initial goal, which is well within reach, but calls for some initiative and personal endeavour.

Children need to be actively encouraged to invite friends into the home to share their interests and activities. This is especially important for an only child or where the interests of children in the family do not coincide. Children need to choose their own friends and any attempt to force young people together with 'suitable' companions is doomed from the start. Parents need to welcome such friends even if they do not particularly like them and they are not the companions they would select for their children. A friend is a very personal choice and feelings can be deeply hurt if this choice is openly criticised.

Cases will arise where a friend, invited home, exerts an influence that is particularly objectionable and perhaps unacceptable to the parents. In this case it would be inadvisable to point this out directly but rather to help the child reach his own conclusions and allow the friendship to lapse gradually. As they grow up, children will have to learn to mix with all types of people. Fussing too much over the calibre of the friends they choose will not always be in their long-term interest.

The Place Of Television As A Leisure Pastime

No discussion on leisure activity or relief from boredom would be complete without considering the place of television. It plays a significant part in most family's lives and often takes up a large proportion of leisure time. It is frequently the chief form of relaxation for parents and, as such, children easily follow suit.

Television is available to all, it calls for no effort and no extra expense however much it is used. Why then is it not the total answer to filling leisure time and bringing ready-made fun for all? The answer lies in the fact that it often offers little challenge to children, since it mostly calls only for listening and watching; it seldom stimulates activity and provides no goal. Young children who sit for hours on end watching, because their parents use the television as a baby-sitter, can get so used to the noise and the flickering screen that they become hooked. It can become an hypnotic that seems to paralyse. Some children find it hard to settle unless the television is on; they know no other form of relaxation and it becomes an obsession, something they cannot live without. Obviously no one wants this to happen.

Some guidelines for viewing:

Gaining self-discipline over watching television lies in setting the right guidelines from the start. Young children readily accept meal-times, bath-time, playtime and bedtime, so 'television time' easily falls into an acceptable time category. They soon come to know their special programmes and with encouragement they will watch only when these are on.

In order to keep up this routine children need to see their parents turning the set off when a programme comes to an end rather than leaving it on as a background distraction. Children also need to see their parents set an example by positively planning their viewing rather than switching on at random to fill time.

As children get older, parents need to discuss the content of programmes with them. Where a particular child is likely to get upset, then watching with parents, rather than forbidding the programme, will cause less rebellion. It is surprising how soon children develop likes and dislikes that suit their temperaments and so are able to choose for themselves quite wisely.

Some unsuitable viewing is bound to occur, but there is a positive side to this. So long as communication in the family circle is good, then sensitive subjects covered on television can stimulate a useful discussion, which otherwise would never come up naturally. Violence and brutality can be put in perspective by emphasising compassion and caring as reflected in other programmes. Titillating sex, crime and getting money the easy way can be offset by comparison with programmes reflecting tenderness, honesty and endeavour.

The existence of television opens up a big responsibility for parents. Through it, via follow-up discussions, values can be passed on to the young casually and naturally. Through the proper use of television this exchange of ideas and values can take place without parents having to make a series of moral issues out of things from which they fondly hope to protect their children. This, of course, applies to such subjects as child molesting, amongst others.

Children have to learn to live in and accept the world as it is, not as we would like it to be. They cannot be protected indefinitely from reality. Even if we wished to do so, we cannot stop other children passing on knowledge of the seamier side of life, and doing so in a much more traumatic way than would be the case through open and frank family discussion.

As children reach their teens there are many programmes from which to choose, offering real educational and entertainment value. The big problem is to avoid the slow drift into too much unproductive viewing. This can allow television to take up all of the family's leisure time, to reduce meaningful intra-family conversation and to discourage many other beneficial activities. The key lies in limiting watching time but this is easier said than done. Bad habits, especially if entrenched, are hard to break. Even these, however, can be replaced by a whole new, more satisfactory regime if it is agreed and acted upon by the whole family.

There must be many ways of doing this, certainly enough to test the ingenuity and tenacity of most families to the full! For example one family decided, after discussion, that television was taking up too much time all round. All agreed it was too tempting to resist by simple strength of mind and that self-regulation without help was too difficult to be successful. The plan they eventually devised called for, as a first step, moving the television set out of the main family room. Anyone who wanted to watch a programme had to make a deliberate move, out of the family circle, to do so. Each child was given a sum of money each week to buy television-watching time. A rate was set on the cost per hour and the money collected in a special money-box. The money and rate were adjusted to allow a reasonable amount of viewing time each week. Each individual could 'buy' viewing time as and when they chose, but once their allocation was 'spent' that was the end of viewing for that week. Certain educational programmes, including the news, were agreed to be free. Money from one week could be saved for another week or could be spent on anything each individual chose. This plan worked and changed four television addicts into three controlled viewers and one complete TV 'drop out'! Family life was much improved in the process. The important clue to success was that the plan was put into operation by mutual consent and not by parental coercion.

Another family grew to dislike the accent on materialism which seemed to grow out of television advertising. They countered this by making a family game out of discussing advertisements and deciding which were successful and which were not. This gave rise to general discussion, developed a critical attitude and brought to light the whole question of suggestibility. The old cry of "Why can't we have . . . ?" was heard less often and then only amid a storm of good humoured protest.

Finally, if viewing is going to be fun, the less it is associated with punishment the better. Threats to withhold popular programmes brings tension and resentment into what should be a fun activity. In fact, denying fun of one sort or another is often used as a convenient form of punishment without its being realised that it is rather like forbidding a child supper if he behaves badly! Fun is a vital emotional food and it is starvation of this food that explains so much restlessness, 'way-out' tastes, boredom and 'kicks' like vandalism, violence, drugs and alcohol.

Finding Pleasure Through The Senses

It is often said that the best things in life are free and this is certainly true of the pleasures available to everyone through the senses. Children need to be encouraged to appreciate this. From an early age they can be helped to notice all the different textures of such things as toys, clothes, furniture, pets, sand, water and so on. They can be helped to find enjoyment in all the wonderful sights, sounds, smells and tastes that are around them. All that is required of parents is that they encourage their children to notice these things and to share their enjoyment of them:

"Oh, these roses look so beautiful and smell so lovely!"

"Feel how soft pussy's coat is."

"Listen! There is the cuckoo."

"The smell of newly baked bread makes my mouth water."

Later children can enjoy, if encouraged, pictures, good writing, poetry, sculpture, striking architecture as well as music and rhythm. There is also so much in nature, even in a city, that is simply taken for granted and chances of endless enjoyment are missed.

Laying The Foundations For A Happy Sex Life

Every healthy person derives pleasure from their body. Small children suck their fingers and toes, clutch at their skin and rub and pull their noses and ears. The genital area is sensitive to touch and holding and rubbing the genitals is perfectly natural in a young child. Parents often worry needlessly over these early explorations, especially if they happen in public or at an age when they feel their child should be beyond doing that sort of thing so openly. When children feel shy, unsure of themselves or bored, they are apt to handle their genitals because this brings a feeling of comfort. It is similar to father reaching for a cigarette when he feels uptight!

Little children are also very interested in, and enjoy examining and playing with, what comes out of their bodies. They have no preconceived ideas on hygiene or offensive smells. To a child urine is simply warm, coloured water and faeces are like squishy mud. In addition, they feel that as these things come from inside themselves, they must be nice! Only adults using such words as "Ugh!" or "Horrid! Don't touch!" and pulling faces, make a child feel his body and its contents are dangerous and dirty.

Pleasure in sex, in adult life, is something all parents want for their children. Whether or not a person finds this pleasure can depend, to some extent, on his early attitudes to his own body, as well as the way his curiosity is satisfied about the facts of sex. What then are the main things that parents can do to make sure that their child grows up with the best chance of enjoying sex in adulthood?

Avoiding arousing guilt about sex

As a start, an interest in sucking, excreting and masturbating is best treated as a normally interesting and pleasurable activity. Children soon learn, by example rather than by scolding, that there is a proper place for the contents of their potty. Real mud and sand are good play substitutes and the idea that messing about with them is acceptable, while messing about with excreta is something that is not done, is soon absorbed as a fact of life rather than a moral issue. Touching the genitals is likely to be short-lived if something interesting to hold or play with is offered when distraction is needed. During the whole of the toilet-training period the child's excreta need to be thought of as good and his body something to be happy about and of which he can be proud. At a later stage, when interest is focused on the other sex and a child gets hold of many smutty rhymes and jokes, care has to be taken not to surround the whole subject with disapproval. "How boring" is a much better response to endless lavatory jokes than "Don't be rude and disgusting".

Guilt can be avoided when answering questions about sex by answering truthfully in language suitable to the age of the child, only giving as much information as is needed to satisfy curiosity. The voice and attitude need to be as matter of fact as when answering any other question. There are many books that give detailed guidance about how best this can be done.

Experimental sex-play with other children is quite common, but often gives rise to a guilt-provoking response from parents. Naturally these sorts of games are best avoided but no one can watch children all the time and games of 'Doctors' or 'Mums and Dads' crop up frequently. Instead of describing these games as "Very naughty", parents can express a firm impersonal limit: "Children do not touch each other's . . . (children's pet name for genitals) because that part is very tender and needs looking after carefully". "But I like doing it!" said a 4 year old with disarming frankness. Her mother sensibly agreed that of course it was pleasant but it simply was not a game that children play. She explained that there were rules about modesty that everyone agrees upon and that these rules are ones that we all agree to keep. The limit may need to be emphasised and repeated but words such as 'disgusting', 'dirty', 'nasty', or 'dangerous because it makes you sick', should be avoided. If a child questions further, then truthful answers are called for, expressed in a matter of fact way.

After 10 years of age a child's sexual awareness begins to develop quite rapidly and parents have again to avoid secrecy or guilt. In fact the age when intercourse becomes a serious question of "Do I or don't I?", is getting lower and lower and as a result early pregnancies are increasing.

The first essential is that children be given all the facts necessary to regulate their ideas and behaviour. These include the plain biological facts about intercourse, pregnancy, contraception and the position of teenagers in regard to the law covering intercourse. This information, in part, is given at school but the biological, medical and legal facts, although essential, are not enough on their own.

Values about sex need discussing

The emotional side of sex is a delicate and complex subject, as are the values connected with it. These values, which vary from family to family, are ones which most parents wish to pass on to their children, especially if they feel they will lead to their long-term happiness. For example, these values may include a wide variety of views on sex as an expression of love and tenderness; as part of a deep and meaningful relationship; sex allied to procreation only; sex as an appetite and source of pleasure; fidelity, pre-marital sex, promiscuity and the value or otherwise of sexual experience and competence.

To have any hope of imparting these values and of having them considered, let alone accepted, by children, parents have to be prepared to discuss between themselves exactly what it is they wish to pass on. They need to discuss how to do this in a way they both accept. Just putting it off and hoping for the best is too risky, but it is the position into which couples tend to drift, even when they know they should do something about the problem.

Once parents have decided what message and values they wish to pass on, there is yet one other vital fact to bear in mind. No one can spring a very complicated set of rules and ideas onto a 10 or 12 year old with any hope of them being digested. No single 'talk' can cover this ground; it needs to be a continuous process and can start soon after babyhood. How young teenagers will behave sexually may well be a reflection of the ideas on modesty, self-respect and willingness to differ from the crowd if need be, which parents have imparted over the years. From infancy onwards our own attitudes and values will be absorbed by our children to a lesser or greater degree, depending on our approach. We should not blind ourselves to our responsibility in this regard.

When trying to pass on values some parents fail to take into account the modern scene, especially when it differs from what they knew in their own childhood. Many shut their eyes to the pressures to which their children are now subjected. Rebellion or guilt may well result if present-day values are derided. Parents all too easily earn the label 'square' from the young and, once this happens, their views are likely to be ignored or their children made to feel ashamed of their freer, modern outlook.

This does not mean that in quiet discussion parents need to give up passing on any deeply-felt views on the subject. They do, however, first need to listen carefully and with sympathy to the modern outlook before putting forward their own more mature ideas. Success in imparting values on sex will always depend on the warmth of the relationship and ease of communication that exists between parents and their children. Criticising, moralising and condescending "I know best" attitudes get nowhere with teenagers. Once a discussion is triggered off naturally, the opportunity to make it as wide-ranging as possible can be taken. Discussing 'dating', 'petting', the Pill, AIDS and VD, long and short term relationships, 'shacking up', 'going steady' and marriage, is the only way in which parents can hope to have any influence. While teenagers may not agree with their parents' views, at least there is a chance the discussion may have some effect on their future behaviour.

Show confidence in a teenager's good sense

Once a son or a daughter starts to go out on their own, it takes courage for parents to show confidence in their child's ability to be sensible. It is sometimes difficult to avoid expressing nagging doubts and anxieties. If this is done it is bound to be self-defeating. The tendency will be for the child to leave home reflecting, to some extent, the attitude of his parents towards him. If he feels they don't trust him he will tend to be untrustworthy; if, on the other hand, he feels they have confidence in his common sense, he will tend to be sensible and justify that trust. The fact is that unless a child is going to be wrapped up in cotton-wool, the parents have little choice but to sit on the sidelines, show trust and confidence, and be ready to pick up the pieces if things go wrong. For the most part they can only hope that their teachings from early days onwards will pay off.

Avoid passing on 'hang-ups'

One mother, concerned for her teenaged children's happiness said, "I can't talk to my kids in an easy, unselfconscious way. Of course I want them to be happily married, but doing anything about it myself seems to be beyond me. I wish I could put them in the freezer until they leave home!".

This mother obviously had 'hang-ups' of some kind. Hang-ups about sex are very infectious where children are concerned. If someone feels guilty about sex themselves, it is very difficult for them to keep out a disapproving and moralising tone when talking about it. This can do a lot of harm.

Once a parent realises that they do have a hang-up it is best that they leave sex education to books, to school, to discussion groups or courses on television organised by professionals. This does not mean leaving everything to chance but it does mean continuing to care and making opportunities for any specialised education that is available. It also means being ready to listen and letting children air their views while making a special effort not to show signs of shock or telling them they should be ashamed of themselves. Sex makes or mars so many lives that it is worth getting professional help on how to get it across to the young if it seems an especially difficult task.

The unwelcome 'fun' which concerns many parents is the involvement of their teenage children with sex, drugs, alcohol and anti-social group activities.

What has been said about sex applies to all these other unwelcome activities. Values and facts have to be instilled from an early age. Reprimands, threats, and lectures once a child is found to be involved, are of little use and can incite further rebellion against parental authority.

The build-up towards teenage common sense and continued response to parents' influence is a continuous process that needs to be started from an early age. Good communication is essential and a vital part is the ability of parents to answer questions calmly. Straightforward facts on all these activities are available in books or pamphlets and these include advice to parents on how to put them over. Values are a different matter and will be personal to each family.

Television provides many opportunities for discussing values and a child is seldom disinclined to talk about the seamy side of life. No confidence shared about their experiences should appear to shock, to be condemned or ridiculed. Any of these will immediately stop the flow of confidences, probably indefinitely.

It is no good shelving responsibility by just hoping that school or the odd book left around will fill all the gaps without any discussion. We are all apt to hide behind an attitude of "It couldn't happen to my child", until it does!

Interests, hobbies and sports involving both sexes always helps. Other acceptable outlets for individuality such as dance, drama, art and music will help to keep reliance on less satisfactory forms of amusement to a minimum.

A happy sex life certainly lends sparkle to living just as enjoyable activities and interests enrich leisure time and provide much-needed relaxation. All work and no play makes us dull and helps build a feeling of discontent and emotional hunger. This is not what we want for our children, so it is worth considerable effort, time and thought, as well as some money, to bring fun and laughter into their lives.

38

CHAPTER 6 : Avoiding The Tension Builders

In the previous chapters it has been suggested that a spirit of cooperation between parent and child is most easily achieved in a calm atmosphere when tension is low. The theme has also been developed that one of the best ways to keep tension down is to keep up a good supply of the basic emotional needs of being loved, feeling successful and having fun. The positive ways in which this can be done have been described.

The Danger Of Spontaneous Comment

It is an odd but interesting fact that many of our most natural and spontaneous comments in response to children's annoying behaviour often do much to negate the good that may have been done in meeting their emotional needs.

These "Doing what comes naturally" reactions on the part of adults are, by their very nature, hard to eradicate or change. Every one of these 'negative', spur of the moment, harsh comments or jibes, chip away at a child's peace of mind and self-confidence. A child, once so deflated, will refuse to communicate except through rebellion or withdrawal. At the same time any hope is lost of settling problems amicably by discussion.

These spontaneous ways of reacting, which are so unsatisfactory, are often relics of an adult's own past experience in his childhood. It is likely that his own mother or father used them in hitting back at him when he annoyed them. However natural it may be, this habit can cause trouble out of all proportion to the temporary relief it brings. It is, therefore, worth breaking.

When parents become angry, one reaction is for them to counter-attack and they do this by moralising, making judgments or offering unasked for advice, and by threatening, ridiculing, ordering, brushing aside or banishing their children. Some examples follow:

"Don't you dare do that again."

"If I were you I would sit still for a bit and read a book."

"Don't bother me now. Later."

"What crazy nonsense are you up to now?"

All of these remarks bring some relief and satisfaction to the parent and certainly make the child feel at a serious disadvantage, but they do nothing to solve the problem that caused all the trouble in the first place. As a result they are self-defeating. Not only do they achieve nothing useful, they do worse than that: they backfire and, as a result, problems build on each other in a self-generating spiral of tension.

Accepting that this will be the inevitable result may provide parents with some motivation to break the habit. Recognising and labelling the commonest of these spontaneous comments also helps to put them where they belong — in the dustbin for the rubbish they are! A description of the worst offences follows:

1) *Moralising, blaming and criticising*

When adults talk to people they consider unimportant and whose opinion they do not value, it often shows in their voice and attitude. They are both careless of the effect of their words and uninterested in what they hear in response. How differently they talk and behave, how attentively they listen, to more important and prestigious folk.

"I'd never do that!" might be the response to such an accusation, but on reflection . . . ? No matter how much parents love and care for their children, they do, sadly, so often put them in the "unintelligent, unimportant" category. They do so at considerable cost to family harmony and to the development of their children's confidence and self-esteem. Children recognise this humiliating approach and like any human, of any age, they react with hostility. Parents who add moralising, blaming and criticising to their "You don't matter" tone add fuel to the fire.

Mother is all concern and charm for the important visitor who has carelessly spilt tea on the carpet, but is scathing to her child who does the same. To her visitor she says, "Think nothing of it, my dear. Accidents so easily happen; it will clean in a jiffy. Here, let me get you another cup". But to her child she says, "Oh, you stupid child. Can't you watch what you are doing? What a mess. Do you think I have nothing better to do than clean up after you?".

What has been achieved by this spontaneous outburst? Plenty, but for the child, all negative. The child will feel hurt, resentful, unloved and angry, certainly in a mood for war, not peace, and anything but contrite.

Spontaneous remarks of a moralising and critical kind are often as untrue as they are impolite. For example, consider a mother's reaction to a child's indignation at the annoying behaviour of a younger brother. Jim says, "I hate Dennis. He is always spoiling my games", and mother retorts, "That's horrid of you. It's wicked of you to say you hate your brother. You know quite well he is a nice boy. Anyway, everyone loves everyone else in the family".

In a cooler mood, the mother will realise that little of what she has said is either fair or true.

2) *Ordering and insisting*

"Do that", "Go at once", "Don't argue", "Do as I say". "Stop this minute", "Shut up, I'm busy". This type of remark is often used as a time saver.

The parent may feel that his time and importance justify such impoliteness, but the effect on the child, unless he is too frightened or cowed, will be to make him want to resist or rebel. These orders and commands have to be shouted louder and louder and more and more often.

Teenagers react particularly strongly. Confidence in themselves and the level of cooperation with their parents will fall steadily under a stream of orders. Added to which, if always told what to do, a child will tend to grow up lacking in initiative, independence and the courage to go it alone. He may be very suggestible and easily become brainwashed by more dominant people's ideas. The "Don't you dare!" approach breeds either revolt or a sense of inferiority and, in either case, breaks communication.

Commands are badly received at the best of times, but when a parent asks of a child a higher standard than he sets himself, then resentment and revolt are magnified. No child takes kindly to being told constantly to tidy his toy cupboard and clothes if his parents' bedroom or father's workshop is usually in a chaotic mess.

So the message is clear. As a general rule, when dealing with children it pays to request – firmly if necessary, but always politely – rather than to command. A little VIP treatment can do little harm and generally does a power of good.

3) *Advising*

This habit couples the giving of a disguised order with the suggestion that "I know best" and implies that "You know nothing".

Examples:

a) "If I were you I would leave that alone."
b) "We are only thinking of your own good. I suggest you work harder if you want to get on."
c) "Robin is such a pleasant lad, you should make friends with him. I'd ring him and ask him round if I were you."

If a child wants advice, and especially if he has asked for it, he will listen attentively when it is given, but if it is thrown at him he will often turn a deaf ear or most likely disagree on principle and retort, "Well you think that's obvious, but I don't agree".

Often the advice may suit only the parent and often it is incomplete. The parents may like Robin, but choosing a friend is the child's problem and maybe he happens to dislike him.

Sometimes a wonderful chance to give assistance is missed, either in response to a call for help from a child or when gratuitous advice that misses the point blocks further conversation. For example: "Jane, how often have I told you not to waste time watching rubbish on TV?" But Jane likes what she is watching and does not find it rubbish at all. She may well think about the rubbish that her parents watch! So she decides that the advice is not only unsound but unreasonable. She is unlikely to follow it and, if there is a row, she may well go to a friend's house and watch her programme there.

If giving uninvited advice raises tension, it obviously needs to be avoided; but what if a child asks for advice? Even then, it is better to avoid giving direct advice, and to try instead to get the child to solve his own problem, albeit with some assistance. Where a parent's opinion is based on sound experience it may help weight the scales in favour of the more sensible solution, and should therefore be passed on. But unless the issue is very clear-cut, the child should not be made to feel that he must follow suit. The advantage of one solution or the other can be stated and the child left to choose.

4) *Name-calling, sarcasm and ridicule*

Dubbing children unkindly, ridiculing them with cutting remarks or making them feel foolish is a sure way to breed resentment and rebellion. It denies their wish for approval and knocks their self-esteem. For example, if you challenge a child with, "You idiot! Haven't you the sense to stir the sauce before it burns?" you are likely to be met with the equally sarcastic, "No, I burnt it on purpose".

Equally, a remark such as "You look absurd in all that make-up", asks for the cheeky response, "So what! It's hardly surprising when I am copying you". This sort of snide jibe allows the adult to let off steam at the child's expense, but invites rudeness and disrespect in return. Some children, not cast in the tougher mould, simply wilt under sarcasm, ridicule or name-calling, and relationships become fraught with tension.

5) *Threats and promises*

Responses to a child's behaviour are often of a threatening or warning nature and could go something like this:

"You'll be sorry if you do that."
"If you behave like that no one will want you around."
"If you do that again I'll give you a good, hard slap."
"Just do that again and see what happens."

Threats of losing love if they do this or that, imply rejection and strike at the very heart of a young child's security. Similarly, threats of fierce policemen, monsters, ferocious wild animals attacking them or hell-fire, are all very damaging as they are concepts against which the child has no defence.

Teenagers, on the other hand, tend to treat threats in the same way as they react to orders and commands. They often scorn them on principle and the parent may easily be faced with retorts of: "You just try", "Nuts", "I couldn't care less", or "That's what YOU think". Even the ultimate threat of banishment from the home or losing the parent's love often has little obvious effect. The teenager's response could be: "I don't care. What good are you to me, anyway?", "I'll get by — I'll manage". The parent is summarily dismissed, family relationships deteriorate and communication breaks down.

Promises often go hand in hand with threats. For example: "Next time you do that I will smack you". This is an idle threat unless it is carried out. If a threat is empty and the child knows it will not be carried out, it becomes totally ineffective and only harms relationships. "Next time you do that I promise I'll smack you" is not much better as the parent may well forget and the child soon learns to ignore threats and to distrust promises.

Promises are sometimes really bribes: "If you are good I will give you a sweet". There are two dangers about this kind of bribe promise. First, the child will always try to 'up the ante' until the promise becomes unreasonable or impossible to fulfil. Secondly, the desire to gain his reward may encourage the child to lie about his actions. Finally, it can be harmful to extract promises from children that parents know cannot possibly be kept. "Promise me you will keep still if I give you a sweet", or "Promise me you won't interrupt again if I let you look at this book". Not even a whole packet of sweets can make a small child keep still and no book printed will prevent a child from interrupting if he needs attention badly enough. Obviously, asking for promises such as these is asking for them to be broken.

6) *Reasoning and probing*

Patient reasoning and logical explanations of a parent's point of view are exactly what a child likes when he is being asked to cooperate. He responds well to being told why, and if the reason is sensible he is likely to agree. At the same time, if reasoning is overdone or used at the wrong moments, it tips the scales the other way. In calmer, quieter moments it has the right effect, but a hurt, resentful child often becomes deaf to reason, and will pick on any extraneous point to challenge so that a long argument ensues.

MOTHER: "No you can't go to the movie tonight because you have school tomorrow. There won't be time to do your homework and getting home late means you will be tired tomorrow."

JOYCE: "I don't want to go to school. We don't learn anything, everyone fools about and makes a lot of noise."

Any further attempt at reasonable discussion will fail. School efficiency, teacher control in class, have all been thrown in to cloud the issue, which is whether she goes to the movie or not. Apart from prompting this diversionary technique that ends in useless argument, the use of logic seems in itself to have the automatic effect of putting an argumentative child on the defensive. The first line of defence is "that's obvious" and from there the child will stubbornly move behind a wall that reason cannot penetrate and from behind which remarks such as "You won't change what I think", or "You can't force me to agree" are hurled.

Attempts at reason and logic also bring the following type of reaction: "My father imagines he is always reasonable. He goes on and on explaining why this, why that, and he is sure he is convincing me. I get so bored. I just switch off and never hear a word".

So, when tension is high, it is often wise to put reasoning aside. A little less preaching and a little more listening could bring better results. If a parent wants to sound out a child's point of view, then the unsatisfactory way to set about it is to bombard him with a battery of questions that smack of interrogation. Trying to probe will put a child on the defensive and far from volunteering the information required, he will tend to fall back on monosyllabic answers that mean nothing:

MOTHER: "Is Bill coming to play?"
JOHN: "No."
MOTHER: "Why ever not?"
JOHN: "Don't know."
MOTHER: "Have you quarrelled with him?"
JOHN: "No."
MOTHER: "Aren't you friends with him any longer?"
JOHN: "You'd better ask him."
MOTHER: "Is he ill? Did his mother stop him from coming?"
JOHN: "Don't know."
MOTHER: "There must be some reason. Are you hiding something?"
JOHN: "Oh, leave it alone! He's not coming and that's it."

Going through John's mind, during this barrage of questions, could be these thoughts: "I won't tell. Why should I?", "Who I play with is my business, isn't it?", "Well, I don't know the answer, so why pester me?", "What a lot of fuss over nothing!", "What is she trying to get at, anyway?".

The type of question that helps communication and tends to keep it going is rhetorical rather than probing:

"How's things? All well?"

"Oh, is that so? And then?"

"Really? It was like that, was it?"

These short questions, showing interest and no more, are an invitation to continue talking, an invitation that is usually accepted. They are part of the skill of 'Receptive Listening' which will be discussed in Chapter 10.

The timing of questions can play a vital part in the type of response obtained. If a mother, for instance, seeing a look of guilty misery on her child's face, asks spontaneously "What's wrong?" and the child is really feeling guilty, the direct question may make him hang his head without answering. Or he may say, "Oh, nothing". On the other hand, if Mother bides her time, shows sympathy by a touch or facial expression, then the child is more likely to feel able to confide and so share what is disturbing him.

Many questions, apparently harmless, are in fact loaded, and make a child feel that a grown-up is trying to trespass on his privacy. For example: "Where did you and Sean go this afternoon?"

"What did Granny talk to you about today?"

"Who did you play with at school or were you all by yourself?"

"What did your teacher say about your homework?"

Children like and respond to interest shown through questions, but it must be clear that genuine interest is the motive and not an attempt to wheedle out information that is private, touches sensitive areas or that is later going to be used against them. So, although questions are an important part of conversation, they should, if a climate of cooperation is to be built up, show genuine interest and be put with tact, while any unwillingness to reply needs to be treated with respect.

7) *Brushing aside or banishing*

When the going gets tough in talking to children, parents often tend to shelve the problem or make light of it with phrases such as:

"Don't worry. It will sort itself out."

"You mustn't make a mountain out of a molehill."

"You are not going to get a rise out of me you know."

"You're only joking I'm sure."

"Let's talk about it some other time. It's not vital is it?"

This playing down or brushing aside what to the child may seem a serious problem is asking for still more trouble. He wants to be heard and his self-respect will be deeply wounded if he is not taken seriously. Similarly, banishing the person as well as his problem is not a good idea. Yet how often does a parent say, "Go to your room and cool down". This is a way of escape which readily comes to the tongue in a crisis and is used by adults to avoid facing an issue and, at the same time, take the stuffing out of a child by asserting their authority. If the child feels he is not wanted or accepted, his self-esteem gets a severe knock. But separation — as opposed to banishment — can be a good idea when tempers and tension are rising and when it is a mutually-agreed process. For example: "I'm off outside. Let's have this out later when we have both cooled down a bit". The response is usually one of agreement. "Perhaps that would be best. I'm so cross I can't even think straight."

When tension has been built up by a quarrel, some release is needed fairly soon, and this is especially true in the case of younger children who, if banished while still upset and angry, may get up to serious mischief as an added complication. The mere act of banishment could easily reinforce existing discontent with more hurt and humiliation and these will tend to swamp any cooling effect the enforced separation might have had. Nothing will be resolved.

When small children have temper tantrums that are upsetting the rest of the family, a parent may decide to remove them, while giving calm reassurance of their affection. Relief is always felt, even if the screaming, hitting and kicking tantrum continues in the face of the calming reassurance. Under such circumstances any physical attack by the child or attempt to hurt the person on whom he depends, must be restrained. If the attack is allowed to succeed, guilt and fear of reprisals will increase the already turbulent feelings. Calm and patience are the clues for the parent, not disregard and isolation.

The child's need for reassurance after a fit of temper is often shown by remarks like these: "Are you sure you still love me?", "I didn't mean all the horrid things I said, I just felt so angry";"I'm glad you didn't let me bite you, though just then I wanted to chew you up into little bits".

For older children, being sent out of the room is less traumatic and also quite ineffective. They treat the whole thing as a joke and even forestall their parents by announcing: "OK, I'm off to my room to play my radio. That's much better than being down here".

To summarise, many of the parental ways of retaliating when tension is running high do nothing in the long run to change behaviour for the better. They only stir up yet more tension and so set up a self-defeating spiral of events.

Most of the weapons that have been described come to hand very easily, but they offer no long-term solutions and can undo much of the good achieved in other ways. These spontaneous reactions may be natural, but we cannot escape from the fact that they produce stress, break communication and land us with more hassle in the end. How easy it is to say "Avoid building tension". But exasperation can mount to such a point that reason no longer controls our actions or words. The knowledge that our spontaneous reaction is self-defeating is overridden by the intensity of wanting to show how much we disapprove. Everyone reaches this point from time to time. There is no need to feel guilty about it, or to feel inadequate as a parent. Instead there is a need to recognise and reinforce the fact that giving way to our exasperation does not pay.

Each time we fail to cool down and explode instead, most of us resolve not to do it again. However, being human, we will be caught off balance again and again. When this happens, once again we remind ourselves that our relief was only momentary, that it soon turned sour as more tension was built up and more unwelcome behaviour had to be faced.

Apart from the spontaneous comments and actions which have just been described, there are other well-known, ready-to-hand methods used in order to try to control the behaviour of children and young people. They include Rewards, Punishment, Rules and Limits. Depending on how and when they are used, they can either increase or decrease tension and so can influence the degree of harmony or hassle experienced in the family. Each of these methods is examined in turn in the next chapter.

The tension-building responses which have been described in the last chapter never fail to arouse resentment and, however tempting it is to use them, they are best avoided. There are, however, another set of responses, which if used correctly can bring useful and positive results. Unfortunately, they are sometimes double-edged, because if used wrongly they can increase tension and promote more hassle.

Rewards

The theory of reinforcement

The theory of reinforcement is well-known and well-tried. It works on the assumption that if a child's acceptable actions are rewarded they will be repeated. With small children, every parent uses reinforcement of good behaviour. Simple useful habits such as greeting people politely, putting shoes away, cleaning teeth and so on, become part of a routine which is willingly accepted if successful attempts have been rewarded. No mother would like to be without the 'reward' weapon. With it she can show quickly and clearly by word, smiles, nods and tone of voice, exactly what pleases her. Her approval is often reward enough. The question then arises as to what other rewards are acceptable and how and when to use them so that the child's good behaviour will be reinforced.

Positive and negative praise

Used in the proper way, words of praise for good behaviour will be accepted by the child as a form of appreciation and reward. In this guise they will bring a sense of welcome attention, pleasure and warmth. Saying what is felt about what has been done well is always acceptable. Mentioning the behaviour rather than sticking a label on the child is infinitely preferable. For example, it is preferable to say, "I see some really tidy homework today" rather than "Clever boy for doing your homework so tidily". Or "I love to see your room looking so nice" rather than "How sensible of you to keep your room so tidy".

To describe a success or to describe its effect is not a difficult thing to do. It is a plain statement of fact. This centres the child's attention on the behaviour approved at that moment.

SELF-EVALUATION can also help to reinforce good behaviour and so can be encouraged with such phrases as: "I like what you have done. Do you?", "Tell me more about how you did that" or "Did you do that all on your own?". This approach helps communication as well as building up self-esteem.

These positive responses to success show adult appreciation, attention and interest. They also give the child the chance to voice what he feels himself. His own satisfaction is the best motive for repeating a successful activity. Being given the opportunity to say "I think I did that quite well — it was

47

pretty difficult" is a far healthier reaction than just being told by someone else that it was a good effort.

On the other hand, certain types of praise can misfire badly. As we all use praise as a form of encouragement, it is as well to be able to tell the difference between successful and unsuccessful praise. The latter breeds rebellion, destroys confidence and breaks communication. Some examples of this negative type of praise follow:

1) *Insincere praise:*

"It makes me mad when mother says that I did that well, when I know it was hopeless."

"When grown-ups try to be polite and say, 'That's great, that's terrific!' and it is over nothing, I just shut up. I feel like telling them to stop talking such rubbish."

Children dislike insincerity. They see it as false flattery.

2) *Praise used as a bribe:*

Children see through this and are likely to react as follows:

"It's no use you telling me I have great musical talent just because you want me to do more practising before my piano lessons."

"I wasn't fooled when Dad told me that I was the only one to get a good shine on the car. I knew what he was after."

3) *Indiscriminate praise:*

If praise is given for every minor accomplishment it soon loses its value. It can give rise to discontent, or a constant hunger for attention. Parents who all too readily deal out praise to a young child, usually tire of it as the child gets older. At the same time the child comes into contact with teachers, friends and peers who are seldom so lavish with their praise. When the expected praise stops, then a dissatisfied feeling of not being appreciated comes to the fore. Self-satisfaction, not praise, should be the motive to succeed. So the quick "Oh, fine. That's a clever girl", or "Well done. That's really terrific", said irrespective of real merit, needs to be avoided.

4) *Praising the person rather than the deed*

Praising a person rather than what they have done can backfire. For example, saying, "What a kind girl you are, Mary, to offer your sweets to everyone" will make Mary feel most uncomfortable if, in fact, she hates the idea of sharing her sweets and is only doing so because she knows she will be forced to do so anyway. In addition, phrases like "How clever you are"may, if repeated often enough, cause a child to stop trying to do better. He could develop a self-image of being sufficiently clever not to need to concentrate or make a big effort. Phrases such as "You are such a good boy not bothering me and playing so quietly" may leave plenty of room for feeling bad when noisy games and demands on mother's constant attention follow. Any personal evaluation lays down a tiresome burden to live up to and an inevitable sense of failure when standards fall. Adrian expressed this clearly when he said, "My mum always says I'm a thoughtful darling when I keep my clothes clean. As I usually get them dirty, she can't think much of me most of the time".

The four types of NEGATIVE praise just described, are all self-defeating and set traps that are well avoided.

Times To Avoid Direct Praise

Direct praise needs to be avoided when children recognise their own mistakes or run themselves down. On these occasions all that is needed is a positive statement rather than acceptance of their stupidity or any attempt to make an excuse for it. For example, a child might say: "Oh, I have been silly and made a mess of this". The positive and helpful response would be: "It's such a help to be able to see one's mistakes as it avoids the same snags coming up next time". While an unhelpful response would be: "It's not really silly — you are usually so sensible".

Teenagers enjoy appreciation but they tend to be a bit sensitive over when and where it is voiced. An admiring glance goes down better than "How nice your hair looks" if it is said in front of friends. Said in private it may bring warmth but, if there is any hint that it means that personal appearance is usually not so good or that a parent is fussing over what is the child's own business, then it is better left unsaid.

So when we are tempted to praise it is better to pause for an instant and make sure it is positive praise and not the negative sort that misfires. The pause can always be filled with an interested, appreciative look, a squeeze or an exclamation of delight, while we search for the right words to avoid coming out with our old brand of negative evaluation.

Treats

Treats given for good behaviour obviously have a place in child rearing. A particularly awkward habit or way of reacting can be helped by the promise of a reward if it is successfully overcome. Treats such as presents, sweets, outings, a special game with Mum, stars on a calendar or many of the other treats rewarding success, can be used to reinforce good behaviour. But when using these material rewards there are certain dangers to take into account.

The Dangers Of Material Rewards

There is always the danger that a material reward, if repeated often enough, becomes the measure of love. The rapidity with which children come to expect presents rather than being satisfied with the deeper pleasure of close companionship, is startling and cause for concern. "What has Daddy brought me?" soon takes the place of the fun of having Daddy back as a companion and friend. "What can I have if I pass my exams?" and "What will you pay me if I wash the dishes?" are the sort of questions that become heard more and more often as the wish for material gain takes over from the wish to please. Once that has happened it is followed by hostility and resentment when money, food or other treats are withheld.

Once you start giving rewards you soon become aware of the ever-growing threat of roaring inflation! One biscuit soon becomes two; tenpence soon becomes a pound; having a friend in soon becomes having the whole gang; and so on to ruin! No one really wants a child to become a taker, looking at people less with affection than for what can be got out of them. It is much safer to emphasise giving and sharing and to reward more by giving attention and love than by giving material things and money.

There is an exception to this guideline that is worth mentioning. Nowadays parents find they have to give their children substantial pocket money. Children make more and more demands because others in their peer group have things and enjoy activities which are now seen as a right for any child. One solution to this constant pressure for more pocket money is to give money for certain jobs that fall outside normal family commitments. Which jobs fall into this 'abnormal' category must be left to each family to decide amongst themselves. This is very different from the bribe offered on the spur of the moment in order to get an unpleasant job done by a child.

Punishments

Useful deterrents

Just as rewards are used to reinforce good behaviour, punishment is used to try to deter bad behaviour. The frown of disapproval, the shake of the head, the short sharp tap on the hand and the firm 'NO' sounding as if it means business, are everyday occurrences when dealing with toddlers. They seem to work successfully as teaching aids and we hardly class them as punishments.

Occasionally, with older children, a stern punishment may be called for if it is a direct consequence of the bad behaviour and follows quickly after the event. It is as well to remember that bad behaviour is often a ploy used by a child to gain attention. Under such circumstances any subsequent punishment becomes a reward in the child's mind and so reinforces the bad behaviour. Taking no notice, rather than punishment, will prove the better way to persuade the child to drop the attention-getting devices that he is using. Naturally the reason for wanting attention is the symptom that needs to be dealt with.

The one form of punishment or retribution that can be used to good effect is one based on the cause-and-effect principle. It is rather more the inescapable result of an action, than a punishment. It has the advantage of being impersonal and so does not effect relationships:

"If I break my favourite toy in a fit of temper, it will not be replaced."

"If I spend my pocket money on things to eat, then I will have to go without other things I want to buy."

"If I am late for dinner without good reason, I will have to get it myself or do without it."

"If I am disobedient when Mummy tells me to do something, then I must expect bad temper and no cooperation from her."

There are sound lessons of life to be learned from this cause and effect process.

The misuse of deterrents

Eye-for-an-eye reprisal, threats, shouting, beating, banishment, withdrawal of privileges or treats, usually have no cause-and-effect connection with the type of misbehaviour encountered. They are all trouble makers not trouble breakers. They seldom bring any lasting changes, and stir up increased tension, fear, resentment or withdrawal rather than regret. Punishment can also set up unwanted values. The eleventh commandment is one. "Thou shalt not be found out." In other words the temporary deterrent is usually coupled with the resolve not to be found out next time, even if this means lying or cheating. Not values to be encouraged!

For sensitive children, the fear and deflation that follows continual punishment may sap their initiative and produce shyness and lack of confidence. In many cases, if severe punishment continues, the memory of the cause, misbehaviour, is banished and resentment conferred on the person who administered the punishment. This is self-defeating as the main purpose of the punishment, to deter, is not realised.

When punishment is over-severe, some children feel so guilty that they invite further punishment to relieve their guilt! Result — more deliberate misbehaviour. As punishment attacks only the SYMPTOM and never the CAUSE of the problem, to serve as any form of permanent deterrent, it has to be repeated but, as the child grows older and stronger and his anger and resentment grow with him, the day may well come when he will counter-attack. The parent then faces defiance to which he has no answer, other than to capitulate or fall back on the biggest failure of all — "Get out and don't come back". For example:

FATHER: "You've been out every night this week. Enough is enough. You are to stay in tonight and do your homework."

TONY: (a tough, well-developed 15 year old): "You can't stop me. Just you try. I'm going out right now!"

And he does just that. Here is another example:

MOTHER: "I will not let you go out in that dreadful dress with three-quarters of your chest showing. Go and change it at once and put on a bra. Plunge lines are not for people of your age."

CHRIS: "What rubbish! You don't know what you are talking about. I expect you want me to wear one of your 1960 models? This suits me fine. I'm off."

For both parents the means to force their wills on the children or stop them were just not there. The long years of punishment now proved useless;

the wish to revolt was uppermost and the power of parents to influence or control was nil.

It may be of interest to look at some other typical results following slapping, beating, scolding, fining, withdrawal of privileges or setting special tasks. Two things are common to these forms of punishment. They usually arouse deep resentment or a need for revenge, because the adult is seen as being totally unfair.

Many parents use the argument that a good slap now and again does help solve the immediate crisis and gets obedience from a child when there is no time for a more complicated approach. They go on to claim that a sound beating can reinforce a lesson to be taught to a naughty child. Whatever the background to their argument may be, it cannot be logical to slap or beat a child into submission and then not expect the child to do exactly the same to his younger brother or sister. There can be no justice in that, and no parent would want a home that accepts hitting and slapping all the way down to the baby.

Taking away privileges as a way of punishment, unless it is a case of direct cause and effect, often fails because there is a considerable time-lag. The offence has been long forgotten by the time the punishment hurts, and so it seems unfair and out of all proportion to the forgotten crime.

Handing out fines can work if it is a case of replacing something deliberately broken or carelessly lost. Unfortunately, until a child becomes self-supporting, pocket money is essential for so many necessities. The result is that more often than not, the parent has to make up the pocket money lost through the fine, in order to meet essentials. If this is not done, there will always be a lurking temptation to steal.

Punishments lose their force unless properly supervised. This is often more bother for the parent than for the child being punished! As Sally remarked to her friend: "Mum made me weed the garden yesterday because I was rude to her. It's stupid really. I just sat around and read a book and, of course, as usual nobody checked. I just said I'd done it and that was that".

Alternatives to punishment

A child cannot be allowed to get away with anything. But if punishment stirs up so much resentment, what are the alternatives? Letting the child experience the consequences of his action is one of them and there are several others.

For example, disapproval can be expressed without attacking the character of the child or knocking his self-esteem:

"It is wrong not to return things you have borrowed", is better than "You are the limit, not returning what you have borrowed".

The effects of discipline on relationships can also be softened by stating clearly the way to make amends and so giving the child the chance to put things right. In addition, pointing out ways to be helpful will encourage the child to solve problems himself and so avoid the need for repeated discipline:

"The paint-brushes could be cleaned and put back in Dad's jar as soon as you have finished with them."

Expectations about how to behave can be put over firmly and clearly but, wherever possible, some choice should rest with the child: "Borrowed things should be returned as soon as possible. Exactly how long you keep them depends on your judgment as to what is fair and reasonable".

Instead of punishing, it is sometimes useful to try to show a child that he has another side to him. He can be shown that he can be self-reliant, obedient and helpful. Expectations can be voiced giving further guidelines:

"I expect you to share your toys."

"Those sweets are for everyone."

"That way of behaving upsets me. Can you try another way?"

"It would be helpful if you learned to dress yourself."

The expected behaviour can also be shown by example, such as responding in a quiet voice when quiet is wanted.

Furthermore, no matter what is said to a child, he will always accept it more readily if it builds up rather than pulls down his image of himself. When he knows he has done wrong, he is far less likely to repeat unwelcome behaviour if he is reminded of better efforts in the past and has something positive to try and live up to. For example, when a child has been particularly thoughtless, Mother could say, "I remember how thoughtfully you helped Jock when he hurt his leg and couldn't get about". Similarly, when a child hears, or overhears, his mother saying something nice about him, he is apt to try and live up to it.

When relationships have been particularly strained and the child is expecting further censure, then, instead of doing the expected, the 'fun' times together can be recalled. This encourages the child to want to restore the cordial atmosphere and make amends.

Every parent needs these reserves to face the thorny problems of day-to-day living. When punishments are doled out for every piece of defiance, then the child begins to take them for granted and learns to get round them if and when he can. So often we punish when already the child is sorry, and to him this is unjust and so deepens discontent. On the other hand, being manipulated by a child who has learned to say an automatic 'sorry' is equally defeating. The challenge to the child of "Well, what are you going to do about it to put things right?" will stop the all too easy apology which has come to mean nothing.

Many of us feel we have failed in our duty if we fail to punish. The following ideas may help to overcome this:

1) We have to expect children to misbehave and so not set our sights too high.
2) We have to accept that much childish behaviour is annoying.
3) We have to realise that the 'eye for an eye' sort of punishment will result in the child thinking "If you punish me, then I will punish you" or "If I am

good, then I should be rewarded". This attitude is what lies behind so much of the egotistical, grab-what-I-can-for-myself approach to life that pervades our society. Most people would prefer their children to grow up turning the other cheek, being understanding of the feelings of others and being ready to make amends when at fault. Our attitude to punishment in the formative years will help determine whether or not they develop these qualities.

Rules And Setting Limits Without Increasing Tension

There is a general reluctance among young people to obey rules blindly whether they are set by the law, by society or by their parents. They may be prepared to comply if they happen to agree with the rule or think it is sensible. Any attempt by anyone in authority to impose a rule with which they disagree, or which they think foolish, is likely to lead to revolt. This tendency to kick against authority applies even to emotionally healthy youngsters, but the reaction will be stronger in the case of any discontented young person.

Defiance of authority is often encouraged by peer groups and, with the strength of numbers behind them, youngsters can cause a lot of trouble. They can show a total disregard for the law and the values of their family. As part of a group, a youngster easily becomes involved in vandalism, drug-taking and drinking, and behaves in ways that no individual would contemplate.

Oddly enough, the same individual, violently resisting the laws of society and home, will obey the strictest rules imposed by his peer group. So the problem is clearly not a simple revolt against all control. It follows that willingness to cooperate is the key to having rules accepted. It is well known that many a teenager, with whom communication is open and relationships warm, will readily discuss the merits of having rules and limits. There is, in fact, a voice amongst the youth of today which supports the idea that when they reach parenthood they will enforce greater control over their children and insist on more social responsibility!

The ways to encourage this cooperation, keeping communication open and relationships warm, are dealt with in Part 3 of this book.

Rules and limits for young children

The position with younger children over enforcement of rules and limits is not as complicated as it is with teenagers. This is just as well as most parents say: "Surely I must make some rules? I must be able to say 'So far, no further' and expect to be obeyed. Surely I must show clearly what I will stand for and what I won't? Surely it is reasonable to say a firm 'No! Don't do that', or 'You mustn't'? Surely there is a place for rules?".

The answer, of course, is yes. There is, however, one 'but'. The setting of limits and rules needs to be done in such a way as to avoid even more hassle.

Many mothers find the toddling stage very trying. It seems to be one long series of 'DON'TS', even if their child is emotionally well-nourished.

Toddlers are up to everything, into everything, making endless demands, crying, dirtying, abounding in energy. As one parent said, "I'll never again criticise a parent for battering her child. One goes mad with saying no, no, no and getting NOWHERE!"

An answer needs to be found as to how to set rules and get them accepted. This should not be too difficult as small children do not like to feel on their own without any direction. They want someone to stop them before they go too far and get into serious trouble. For example: Michael, aged 6, said: "I don't want to go to Simon's house. Anyone can do as they like there and someone always gets hurt".

Susie, aged 3, was playing with her kitten when it scratched her: "How dare you, you horrid thing", her anger flared and she flung the cat across the room. Its back hit a stool and it was paralysed. Susie was inconsolable and at once blamed her parents. "You could have stopped me being so nasty", she said. "Now look, my kitten may die." It was as if she claimed that if they loved her they would never let her do such a wicked thing.

We often meet examples of a young child asking for help to keep out of trouble. Children want an ally against the consequences of their own dangerous behaviour. Especially they do not want to be allowed to hit or hurt the people on whom they depend for love. Children also wish to know what is expected of them so that they can feel confident that they fit in. They usually learn this by copying their parents and by absorbing both good and bad values from those around them, rather than by being given strict rules to follow.

It is possible, with young children, to express a few definite limits in a way which will be accepted and which will lower rather than build up tension. This does not mean overdoing rules. There are some limits that are there for a child's own safety and these brook no argument, but many other personal limits, set by parents, need to be kept to a minimum.

How To Keep Personal Limits To A Minimum

1) *Saying no*

Many of us spend our time saying NO when children are young. In the long run this certainly seems to increase tension. There are alternatives to the never ending stream of NO's that are worth considering.

A moment's pause can be taken before coming out with a firm NO. For instance, saying "Let me see. I'd better think about that" before refusing, helps to soften the blow. Then YES can sometimes be used to replace NO. As an example: "Yes, you can go over and play with James, but after lunch", rather than "No, not now, lunch is ready". Reflecting the child's wishes and using positive limits to control behaviour will also avoid the direct NO. "You want to take all the books out of the shelves. I know it is fun, but books stay in bookcases where they belong when they are not being read." Giving reasons can also take the place of NO. For example: "Books are not playthings because they get spoiled". A child can be told facts that supply information. The NO is then only implied. "These books belong to Daddy." In such circumstances a look or shake of the head will often be enough and so replace saying NO.

A youngster often knows that something is forbidden and he merely tries it on to test his parent's reaction. A firm NO may invite rebellion, whereas a long straight look that sends the same message leaves the choice up to him and he will often comply.

2) *Using time as a natural limit*

The idea of time can be a great ally if it is introduced as an impersonal factor against which no one can argue. "A time for everything" fits the general liking for routine, and knowing what is going to happen next. This is a rhythm a child likes for the sense of security it brings. If rest time, bedtime, meal-time, playtime, bath time, follow a regular known pattern, it can save endless friction and a spate of personal limits in the first three years. "You and me alone time", "Mummy and Daddy's time alone together", "Television time", and "Play by yourself time" can all be put over as a regular way of life. In this way a feeling that time is shared out fairly and that more than a fair share cannot be demanded becomes readily accepted. All these areas of time abound in their own limits, but these can be kept to a minimum by constant routine.

Bedtime is no exception and the following example may help to illustrate the value of not breaking this routine. The example is in the form of a transcript from a tape recording sent by an exasperated mother:"Bedtime has been a running sore, a nightly nag and sometimes a nightmare! Joan demands I stay with her and if I don't she screams and jumps out of bed. She wants a drink, the loo or some other excuse. I know it is my fault. I let routine go by the board. We had a stream of visitors, Hugh's mother came for a long stay, then measles, followed by a caravan holiday. Joan stayed up until all hours and now we are paying the price. Last week, at the end of his tether, Hugh walloped Joan, and we seemed to get into a worse mess. Anyway we took your advice and tried to work out WHY we were having all this trouble. We decided we meet her basic needs. She is cheeky and self-confident and I suppose we spoil her. She is a pastmaster at letting her lip come down before the tears come. We have talked it over and Hugh agrees Joan gets round me too easily. I laugh, when I should be serious. I say NO, DON'T and YOU MUSTN'T all day long, but I'm not firm enough and I often give way. I give her a chance to see the chinks in my armour and she always slips through.

So we decided to explain to her about 'times'; her time and our time. I'm going to see she doesn't sneak off to sleep after lunch, even if it kills me. I will make it clear that saying goodnight is our business, but going to sleep is hers. She can have her books and dolls if she wants them. She'll agree all right, she always does and then quickly breaks the agreement. This time — no way! Both of us feel you are right — even if it means a week or two of struggle. Once she knows she is a party to the bargain and can't slide round it, we may get a routine going instead of a nightly battle. We'll have people in to bridge and avoid going out until things settle down." (Three weeks later) "It's ages now and the tape is still not finished, so here goes. I can hardly believe it but we have won the bedtime saga! At first she strode out getting drinks and grumbling, but making her feel responsible and sticking to routine clinched it. As you suggested we were firm but loving and it certainly worked."

3) *Child-proofing the house*

Another way parents can reduce the need for limits is by child-proofing the house. This means as a first step, putting precious things out of reach, fixing door-catches high up and securing cupboards. A child needs a place to play, a place to mess, clothes that he can dirty and lots of inexpensive toys, which in the course of time he can damage without dire consequences. If a child's space is respected then he is more likely to respect other people's. Most homes can provide a box in which to leave muddy shoes, a bag for his own toilet things and his own towel so grubby fingers do not dirty everyone else's. Expensive carpets and furniture-covers are cause for concern, serious enough when children are older, but a continual nightmare when they are small and climbing over everything with sticky fingers. The less there is to spoil, the less a mother has to keep saying DON'T and NO.

4) *Distraction and substitution*

A third method to decrease the "Leave that, put that down, be careful" process is distraction and substitution. Attention can be switched to something less dangerous, although equally interesting. A sharp knife can be replaced by a big spoon. All mothers do this but it is surprising how often they shout "Don't. Be careful" first. A young child's attention is fleeting and success is assured if a parent uses his imagination and perserverance to by-pass trouble.

5) *Warn of changes in routine*

The fourth aid to avoiding too many limits is to warn children about changes in routine, if possible well in advance. The possibility of a parent going to hospital, a visit to the dentist or doctor, the advent of a new baby, visitors coming, starting nursery school, a new baby-sitter, even plans for a holiday, anything which is outside the accepted pattern of existence, needs to be ventilated and discussed. These events are the nucleus of "I won't" and "I don't want to", in response to which yet more rules get laid down. A child is being invited to rebel or grumble if he is not prepared or forewarned.

Preparing a child for acceptance of a change in routine is not difficult. Anxiety can be allayed well in advance if he is warned about what to expect and is sure in his own mind that he can cope. Often the best way to achieve this is by playing or acting out all possibilities. For example, weeks before nursery school started Rebecca and her mother played at saying goodbye, getting on the bus, meeting the teacher, undressing for swimming, getting into line and so on. Many of the strange activities were rehearsed. When the actual day came, she was used to waving goodbye and the reality raised only a ripple of anxiety.

How To Get Limits Accepted

Even after the most drastic cutting down, there will always be a need for some NO s and DON'Ts and the important question remaining is how to get these accepted without building up further tension.

Children like a firm statement that leaves no room for doubt: "Playing with gas is dangerous. Only grown-ups turn gas on". Children also prefer an impersonal limit that can be repeated again and again without it sounding like a parent's nagging opinion. Examples of some impersonal limits are: "People are not for hurting" instead of "You must not hurt people". "Those flowers are not for picking" rather than "Don't pick those flowers". It is worth noting that children are more likely to accept a choice rather than a specific limit from which there is no escape: "Would you like cereal or an egg this morning?" instead of "You must eat breakfast".

An alternative time or place can also be introduced to make a limit more acceptable. For example: "I can't listen now, but I will later". Or "Be as cross as you like at home, but not now in the street in front of all these people".

In setting limits parents need to keep their cool and to go on repeating them as long as is necessary. If limits are kept to a minimum and all possible steps taken to get them accepted, then they can play a valuable part in reducing hassle, especially in the first few years.

Three factors that encourage emotional satisfaction and a peaceful family life have been described. A multitude of other factors that tend to disrupt this peace have also been mentioned. It now remains to put it all together and set out clear guidelines on how to react in order to take the heat out of stressful situations.

Following a seminar on 'Parenting' several mothers discussed the effects of discarding all the tension-raisers, the old well-tried weapons like threats, name-calling, unasked for advice and punishment. Their comments went like this:

"I'll feel absolutely defenceless. My kids will trample all over me."

"What on earth am I to do if I can't use my usual disciplinary methods? Just let things rip, I suppose."

"I might get hoarse shouting at Tracey, but at least she listens momentarily once she knows I mean business and she feels a good hard slap on her bottom."

They all agreed that when their children were young, they were either cowed into submission or became more agressive when faced with threats, punishment or blame. They also agreed that with older children they were met with cheek, argument, direct refusal to obey or downright dishonesty. Once children were in their teens, it seemed there was little that could be done to force them to comply. In spite of this, they found it difficult to discard the old self-defeating ways of reacting to bad behaviour.

They agreed their old methods allowed them to let off steam so at least THEY felt a bit better even if the children felt far worse! One response came from all of them — a cry from the heart; "Of course it is sensible to give up the old ways, but what do we put in their place?". A fair question that needs to be answered.

The Critical Moment Of Choice

At an early stage in each tussle between parents and children there comes a critical moment, a parting of the ways, where two paths of action are open. One leads to mounting stress and soon develops into a self-generating cycle of increasing tension and discontent. The other leads to more understanding, less tension and finally a willingness to talk, to listen and cooperate.

The diagram (*see page 60/61*) shows both the lead up to the all-important parting of the ways and what happens down each of the separate paths. Like all diagrams, it is a bit limited in scope. It tells less than the whole story but, in spite of this, it can be of use as a simple summary of the problem and its solution. It is labelled in terms of friction arising between parents and their children but the principle demonstrated can apply equally to confrontation between adults.

At its base the diagram shows the point where trouble starts, when

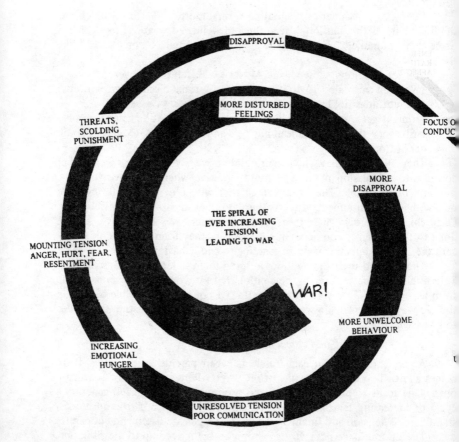

WAR
and
HASSLE

DISAPPROVAL

MORE DISTURBED
FEELINGS

THREATS,
SCOLDING
PUNISHMENT

FOCUS O
CONDUC

MORE
DISAPPROVAL

THE SPIRAL OF
EVER INCREASING
TENSION
LEADING TO WAR

MOUNTING TENSION
ANGER, HURT, FEAR,
RESENTMENT

WAR!

MORE UNWELCOME
BEHAVIOUR

INCREASING
EMOTIONAL
HUNGER

UNRESOLVED TENSION
POOR COMMUNICATION

WHEN TH

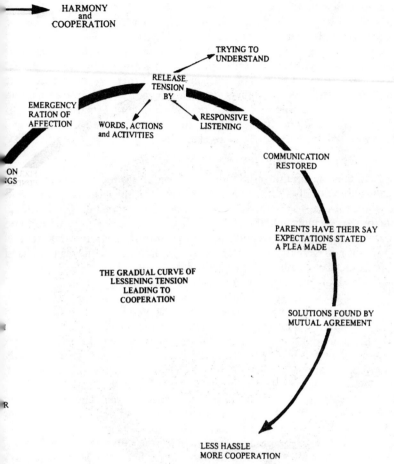

HARMONY
and
COOPERATION

TRYING TO
UNDERSTAND

RELEASE
TENSION
BY

EMERGENCY
RATION OF
AFFECTION

WORDS, ACTIONS
and ACTIVITIES

RESPONSIVE
LISTENING

COMMUNICATION
RESTORED

ON
GS

PARENTS HAVE THEIR SAY
EXPECTATIONS STATED
A PLEA MADE

THE GRADUAL CURVE OF
LESSENING TENSION
LEADING TO
COOPERATION

SOLUTIONS FOUND BY
MUTUAL AGREEMENT

R

LESS HASSLE
MORE COOPERATION

VE, SELF-ESTEEM
ARTS TO RISE

someone is deprived of their emotional needs. Where there is emotional hunger, tension starts to rise and a feeling of discontent is the inevitable result. No matter how wise or devoted parents may be in providing the right emotional food, life itself, with all its frustrations, is likely to leave a few 'hunger pangs' which will give rise to small areas of discontent. The greater the degree of deprivation, the greater will be the degree of dissatisfaction.

In most people, inner discontent shows itself in the form of disturbed behaviour – the symptom. Normal ups and downs, resulting in healthy misbehaviour, can be taken by parents in their stride. If there is serious discontent and it shows itself by behaviour which ruins the peace of the home, then the alarm sounds and the parents are alerted. Something is sufficiently wrong to call for positive action. It is at this point that the choice has to be made. Which way? War or peace – Hassle or Harmony?

The Way Towards War And Hassle

On the diagram this is the fork to the left. This is the path that many of us take automatically. When a child misbehaves it is the most natural thing in the world to react to his CONDUCT and we tend to forget or ignore the reasons for that conduct. We thus take the first step on the path to trouble and are committed. The first reaction of most parents when faced with a troublesome child is to scold, blame, moralise or threaten, to use the ready-to-hand weapons already described. For example:

"You know perfectly well that it is all your fault."

"How can I love you if you are so naughty?"

"If you go on being such a pest, I shall slap you."

"How dare you hit your brother. You are a wicked girl."

These disapproving remarks, the second stage on the path towards trouble, not only add to the child's discontent, but make him feel unfairly treated and that his problem is not understood. Feelings of anger, hurt, resentment and fear well up in him, all of which increase tension. More discontent breeds more misbehaviour and the spiral of ever-rising stress is set in motion. The child rapidly moves into a state of mind where he is quite deaf to reason and refuses to communicate. Tension quickly builds up on both sides. The ability to compromise fades, and misbehaviour not only continues, but can break out more violently and more often. Sooner or later the parent's patience will snap and he will deal out the threatened punishment. His motives will usually be mixed; he will tend to lash out, giving vent to his frustration, but hoping that the punishment will drive home that misbehaviour does not pay. Another step is taken down the path towards blocking communciation and stirring up more resentment. The exchanges between parent and child may go something like this: "How many times have I told you not to do that? Are you deliberately trying to annoy me?" A sharp slap follows with the hope that it will make the child listen.

One of two things could now happen. Depending on the child's make-up, he may be temporarily cowed into submission and a false peace may prevail for a while, but resentment will be simmering; on the other hand, he may react angrily and give immediate vent to his feelings by screaming, kicking and shouting back.

"You are unfair, you're horrid to me! I hate you!"

Even less options are open to the parent now. Is it to be a stony silence or a slanging match? In either of these circumstances tension will increase and, referring once again to the diagram, we move round through "increasing emotional hunger" and inevitably, towards "more unwelcome behaviour".

The war is on! The only question remaining is who will win and who will lose? Nothing is solved. Whoever wins, it is certain there will be no progress, except in a negative direction. Nothing has been done towards indentifying or removing the real cause of the trouble. The punishment and angry words will only create further discontent, which will fester away under the surface.

Bottled-up anger, or any of the other turbulent emotions, will continue to exert pressure; tension will build up and another bout of trouble will only be a matter of time. It may be weeks or only a few minutes away, depending on many varied circumstances. The certainty is that another explosion will occur. The possibility of reaching an amicable or permanent solution fades further away. The 'war' goes on and, like all wars, goes on much longer and becomes more bitter than was ever thought possible.

Parent and child are now well and truly launched on a path of confrontation and, inevitably, the home becomes a less happy and less secure place to live in. There must be a better way. The fork to the right on the diagram is well worth exploring.

The Alternative – The Way To Peace And Harmony

Once again, back to the diagram and the parting of the ways. The situation is as before. Parents have been alerted that something is sufficiently wrong with home relationships to call for positive action on their part. When faced with the next instance of repeated misbehaviour, they take a vital decision: they try to ignore the annoying conduct and they focus their attention on what is setting off the trouble – the FEELINGS that trigger off the child's hostile actions.

This decision sets the parents moving down a new path; one that leads to a lessening of tension and a cooling of tempers and, most important, one which keeps communication open and leads to a point where cooperation comes willingly. Mutually-agreed solutions to problems can then become a real possibility.

The new way is not easy. To reach its goal a number of new skills have to be used. For convenience, these skills will be described in the order shown on the diagram. In practice this may not always apply. There is, in fact, no

63

special order of progress down the path. One sequence may be better with a child of a particular age and temperament, while another may suit better under different circumstances. Experience, backed by intuition, will soon become a useful guide.

For the sake of clarity and better understanding of the new concepts, the steps on the diagram will be demonstrated by a simple example:

Roger, aged 4 years, was always hitting his younger brother. His mother was concerned over toddler Bill getting hurt. So, when the next incident occurred, she carefully avoided slapping Roger, shouting at him or telling him how naughty he was. Instead, she focused her attention on trying to understand why he felt so angry and vindictive towards his little brother. In doing this, she FOCUSED ON FEELINGS. She then set about REDUCING TENSION in all the ways depicted in the diagram.

First she restrained Roger firmly, but gave him a comforting squeeze to show him she cared for him even if she did not approve of his attack on Bill. This represents her EMERGENCY RATION OF AFFECTION. She then made the obvious guess about his feelings and expressed this as: "I think you feel very cross with Bill". This showed Roger that she was trying to understand.

(A detailed explanation will be given in Chapter 9 on how to focus on, identify and understand feelings. This process is not always as simple as it sounds, but in this first vital step lies the secret of heading towards cooperation rather than rebellion.)

To continue with the example. Roger, realising that he now had a receptive ear, readily explained how angry he was and described some of the dreadful things he would like to happen to Bill. Obviously feelings were still running high and more release of tension was needed, but at least Roger felt that someone was trying to understand and was beginning to feel better and more ready to comply. He would at least take some notice of what was being said, whereas in a rage, with tension running high, a parent might just as well talk to a brick wall.

Roger's mother encouraged him to go on talking by using the skill of RESPONSIVE LISTENING. This entailed using her knowledge of the two children, listening to Roger's point of view, paraphrasing it and reflecting it back to him like this: "You are telling me that you feel Bill is always in the way and that he is a nuisance. He takes up too much of my time". Roger continued to explain how unfair he felt this was and his mother gave him full rein to go on talking. She also continued to show him that she was TRYING TO UNDERSTAND his point of view. This skill of responsive listening is dealt with in detail in Chapter 10. It is a skill all parents need to acquire, as it is the quickest and most effective way to take the heat out of any tiresome or explosive situation.

The longer Roger was allowed to let off steam by expressing his anger and resentment in harmless ways, the calmer and more reasonable he became. In Chapter 11 many ways are described to encourage this RELEASE OF TENSION THROUGH WORDS, ACTIVITIES AND PLAY. These outlets are the ones parents need to encourage in order to enjoy reasonably peaceful co-existence within the family.

Once Roger showed the first signs of a willingness to cooperate, his mother explained HER WISHES, feelings and expectations of his behaviour, all backed by HER REASONS.

(How to encourage a child to listen and how to put over the adult point of view is described in Chapter 12, which is headed PARENTS NEED TO HAVE THEIR SAY – CHILDREN NEED TO LISTEN.)

The decision whether to comply or not is left up to Roger. This in itself prevents a resurgence of stress. If he does not comply with adult expectations, then it becomes a subject of negotiation. An enforced solution, even at this stage, has little chance of standing the test of time.

(Chapter 13 deals with FINDING SOLUTIONS BY MUTUAL AGREEMENT. This is a process that can be used with children of all ages and the chapter shows how negotiations as a family, or between two individuals, play an important part in reducing everyday irritations over disagreements.)

Roger's mother would set the negotiations in train in this sort of way: "You feel angry over Bill taking up so much of my time. When you hit him, you are showing him and me, how angry you feel. I have explained that hitting cannot be allowed. People are not for hurting. What do you suggest we do about all this?". Surprisingly perhaps, even a 4 year old is able to make a lot of suggestions and amongst them there is sure to be at least one over which the parent can negotiate and come to an agreement. In the end, Roger suggested: "I would not hit Bill if he played over there on his own with his own toys and you promise to play with me as much as you do with him". Roger's self-esteem had been given a boost by finding a solution. His mother had listened to him. He is far less likely to break the pact that he has suggested himself, especially one which, if broken, will have results which have been discussed and to which he has agreed. It is essential to follow up any mutual agreement with a discussion on what is to happen if either person breaks his side of the bargain!

In practice, it needs to be remembered that reducing stress is not a case of step by regimented step but a much more subtle, back and forth process, playing things by ear rather than by rule.

A further example is given to demonstrate, in a practical way, the whole process of reducing tension and to show quite clearly the difference when the path to 'war' is taken. This example is in the form of an actual situation when each of the alternative paths are contrasted.

A mother, who was having trouble dealing with her son James, aged 8 years, sent this tape asking for help. "You asked me to describe any one incident in detail and say how I dealt with it. There are so many difficult times. They are never the same, except that they all cause trouble and worry. I despair of ever getting on top of the situation with James. Well, this is what happened this morning. I was in the living room, James was making a castle or something on the front paving stones. A frightful mess, mud everywhere! He was covered in it, but he was playing so happily I decided to leave well alone. Suddenly I caught sight of an elderly woman coming to our gate. I saw her hesitate before standing bang in the middle of a pile of mud and leaves. Everything happened in a flash. James cried out and made a grab at the woman's leg, mud smeared her nylons. She shouted at him and he shouted back. I saw him pick up a handful of mud and fling it after her as she reached our front door. As I arrived outside she had her hand raised to clout him and I couldn't blame her. I apologised as best I could. I told James he was a disgrace, that I was ashamed of him and disgusted at his behaviour. I told him to say sorry. He refused. He looked furious and was almost crying. I said again that I insisted he say sorry, but was only met with sullen silence. I then ordered him up to his room and told him to clean up and stay there until I came up and dealt with him. He didn't move at once so I gave him a fairly hefty smack on the backside and that got him going. He really looked a sight with his tears making muddy streaks down his cheeks!

I think I managed to pacify the woman, who I discovered was collecting for the blind. We cleaned up her clothes and I gave her a cup of tea and an extra 50p to salve my conscience.

Then I went upstairs. There was chaos, an absolute pigsty. James kicked out at me when I went up to him and, if looks could kill, I would be dead! He refused to listen to anything I had to say. I've forgotten what I did say as I was as furious as he was. Anyway the gist of it was that I wouldn't tolerate him behaving like an animal and he couldn't have lunch until he apologised. He snorted that he didn't want lunch anyway — why should he say sorry when the woman had wrecked his castle. I said it was bad luck, but no excuse for throwing mud at anyone. He said he wished he had thrown the whole castle at her, and me too. I was a horrible mother. I thought he was going to start kicking me again so I went out. I heard him lock his door and now, let me see, it's over five hours since he has eaten or spoken. I've been up from time to time and asked him to unlock the door and left some biscuits. He has not touched them. I am crazy to have left the key in the lock. I've begged him just to admit that he had behaved badly — only silence.

My neighbour, who saw and heard what went on, popped round and said how good to see that I didn't stand any nonsense. But where has it got me? The whole stupid incident has now blown up out of all proportion. James is so damned obstinate he could keep this nonsense up and, even if he unlocks the door, nothing is solved. Just one more row will be on the way.

Please, please tell me where I go from here? I know I am hopeless at oping, but if I go on much longer like this I will come to the end of my ether. Unlike before, I really am ready to listen, so please tell me what you would have done under the same circumstances? I so badly want some guidelines to get me out of this mess."

James's mother had sent the tension cycle whirling. She was set on a collision course. Obviously everything she said and did made the child more angry, everything he did made her more annoyed and desperate. Her threats were self-defeating, she could see no way to find a satisfactory solution because both had dug their heels in. The following transcript is part of the tape sent in reply, answering her plea for help:

"I can only guess what will be happening when you get this tape, but it seems fairly likely that the atmosphere will be tense. The suggestions that I am going to make are aimed at lowering the tension so that you can talk to each other and break out of the 'everything going from bad to worse' situation. When things have cooled down you may be in a better position to find a solution and close the incident. It will also be easier to think about how to avoid a recurrence.

First then, in whatever way James is reacting, tell him that you have been thinking and that you didn't altogether understand his side of what had happened. Tell him you now want to listen and try to understand. Be sincere about this. Reassure him that it isn't a trick, you love him and that you are unhappy that there is a row going on that is separating you. Persist in showing your interest and wish to understand until he tells you his side. Let him rant and rave. Just listen, avoid defending the woman or yourself.

Then, second. When he has told you his side, try to sum up how he felt and is feeling now. It could go something like this:

"You must have taken a lot of trouble building that castle. How infuriating to see it all broken. You felt the lady deserved to be splattered with mud because she was so careless. Perhaps it seemed to you that she should say sorry to you and not you to her."

This is not agreeing with what he did, but after hearing what he has to say, it is merely showing that you grasp why he did it. Trying to put yourself into his shoes will not only cool James down, but will also help you too.

Third. When James has really talked the problem through, the atmosphere is likely to be calmer and you may find him ready to listen to how you felt at the time. Avoid attacking him. Merely state your expectations positively, something like this:

"I feel very uncomfortable when I see a visitor treated unkindly, even if they have been thoughtless. I put great store on being polite and helpful to people, especially strangers who have come to our home."

Be careful to avoid the demand 'YOU MUST' be polite to visitors, as this takes the decision out of his hands and encourages more rebellion. James may retort that slapping him or punishing him wasn't fair or kind; he, after all, is in the home and that makes it worse. Avoid getting embroiled in arguments or excuses and go back to the fact that you wish you had understood how he had felt. If this sets him talking again, so much the better. It all goes to cool things down even more.

Lastly. If you get the opportunity, put an arm around him and ask him what he thinks is a solution, so that the trouble won't happen again. Consider all his suggestions, even if some sound silly. Perhaps add some yourself and ask James what he thinks of them. BOTH of you decide on the best solution and agree to abide by it. When this is done show how pleased you are that the matter is now settled and mention that there are better ways to settle things than to have rows.

Your second question, as to what I would have done, is partly answered because I would have followed the same course as I have now suggested to you. I would have followed it from the start by understanding James's feelings and so tried to avoid the build up of antagonism.

At the time I would have put a restraining but loving arm around James. I would have tried to verbalise why he felt so mad and would have offered help in restoring the castle later. The damage was done over throwing the mud and while James was feeling so worked up, I wouldn't demand an apology. I would wait until he had cooled down before putting over how visitors should be treated. Naturally, like you, I would have been apologetic to the lady and do all I could to repair the damage to clothes and pride! After she left, I would let James blow off a bit more steam, not agreeing or disagreeing, but just listening. The child's cooperation will not be forthcoming until he has cooled down. Understanding how he feels without criticising, opens up the possibility that he will himself admit his behaviour was not correct. This is a real advance on behaving well just for fear of being punished.

You may wonder what is meant by finding a solution. A pious hope of always being polite to visitors, even when provoked, is unlikely to appeal! A possible solution could be to make castles somewhere less vulnerable.

If James really feels you are trying to help, some compromise will present itself. Silly solutions such as putting 'keep out' notices on the gate can be joked about rather than called stupid. A query such as "Would it help if you did your modelling elsewhere so it won't get spoiled?" would at least leave the choice to James.

I expect when you hear this, you will say how obvious it all is and how easy to be wise after the event! Please, don't feel badly about it. Most people would react just as you did. A whole new approach takes time and practice before it comes naturally — as it will if you give it a chance . . ."

On reading this example parents may say: "It sounds fine in theory, but who has the time in a busy working day to go to all the trouble to solve one silly little crisis, especially when there might be several each day?". In answer to this, two points can be made.

First, the explaining of this plan makes the process much more laborious than it really is. In fact, the whole thing would only occupy a few minutes. The mental effort, too, becomes easier with practice and soon becomes second nature once the skills have been mastered.

Secondly, the time spent will be well spent. It will lead to a closer continuing relationship. Hours of time might otherwise be wasted in continual wrangling that achieves nothing but jangled nerves. Each time a solution is found, it will be easier to stop a recurrence because the sort of trigger that sets it off will become clearer.

These, then, are the options opened up by the alternative paths to follow in every family crisis, large or small. No instructions are needed to follow the path to war. Sadly, it comes all too naturally to many of us. To follow the path to peace requires a good deal of new thinking, practice and perseverance. Like any new technique it may appear overcomplex at first, but with practice and, as the skill develops, it soon becomes straightforward and automatic.

Who has not been through this process when learning to drive a car? Brakes, clutch, gears, switches, signals, other traffic and road signs all present a bewildering collection of actions that have to be co-ordinated at once. As each lesson progresses, they all slot into place until driving becomes quite easy and effortless. In the same way, taking the path towards peace becomes progressively easier. Most of us accept the benefits of skills in dealing with practical everyday problems. Surely the same applies to skills that help deal with the emotional crises that occur from time to time in any home? The effort to learn these skills must be worthwhile if they help to restore calm when bad tempers arise.

Part 2 of this book deals in detail with the skills that are needed to reduce tension and find agreed solutions. When we are at the moment of decision on how to act, these skills will undoubtedly help us to make the right choice, and take the path leading towards harmony and away from hassle.

PART 2 WARMING RELATIONSHIPS AND COOLING TEMPERS

CHAPTER 9: The Skill Of Focusing On Feelings

It Is Not Easy

Focusing on feelings is difficult. It is not as natural as reacting to behaviour It calls for a conscious effort of will. It is easy to express how we ourselves feel in moments of heightened stress. It is much more difficult to guess how another person feels. For instance, if a child is annoying us by crying, we express our annoyance without stopping to think. We wish him to stop and tell him so: "Oh, do stop crying. You're driving me mad".

It needs a conscious effort to ignore our own reactions and make the switch to concern over how the child is feeling. Is he afraid? Is he angry? Does he feel rejected? These are the questions that need to be uppermost in our minds, rather than "I hate it when he cries, I feel so helpless".

Making the switch becomes even more difficult if we are feeling tense and so blinded by our own emotions. The process is complicated further if we are a reserved sort of person who finds dealing with feelings of any kind a strain and would prefer to avoid the whole subject.

In the face of all this, many claim that focusing on feelings requires too much effort and is too difficult for everyday use. Those who say this need to face up to what the alternatives offer. The quick slap, stern criticism or uncompromising order may bring temporary results but they offer no lasting solutions to persistent problems.

Excuses for putting off difficult tasks are always easy to find. We all need a bit of advice and practice before we can bake a cake or change an electric plug. Like any other skill, that of focusing on feelings needs to be worked at before it will happen automatically. One final objection needs to be dealt with before going on. Some people have difficulty in accepting the fact that showing UNDERSTANDING of children's feelings IS NOT CONDONING their behaviour, or giving them their own way. A child may tell a lie out of fear, and making allowances for that fear does not mean accepting or condoning lying. The first things we need to learn are ways to overcome the difficulty of making the switch from "I wish", "I feel" to "WHAT DOES THE CHILD FEEL?"

Begin By Labelling Feelings

The first aid to learning how to focus on feelings is to label them. This is best done by making a list of one's own negative or uncomfortable feelings which have been experienced at one time or another. A second list should be of feelings observed in those close to us. A wide range of emotions will now have name-tags.

This identifying and labelling of all the many shades of feelings avoid the unhelpful tendency to group emotions together. For instance, the terms feeling low, unhappy or annoyed give no depth of insight, whereas if someone says they feel lonely, unsuccessful or unfairly treated, the true position immediately becomes clear.

In the following example a simple statement made by Joyce on return from school, is examined in terms of how she feels. Labelling these feelings and taking all of them into account brings real insight into her problem: "I had the usual wretched morning. My maths went all wrong, Mr Smith even complained my work was messy. I try so hard but I just don't see what goes wrong. Anyway maths is a useless subject, it isn't worth the effort. I'll never use it after school". Analysing this statement we get:

Joyce is feeling a failure – ("the usual wretched morning")
She is feeling resentful – ("Mr Smith EVEN . . .", inferring that he is unfair)
She is discouraged – ("I try so hard . . . to no avail")
She is frustrated – ("I just don't see . . . ")
She is tempted to give up – ("It isn't worth the effort")

If Joyce's parents failed to consider her feelings they might well have responded to her general moan by saying how vital it was to work harder and be neater. In doing so, they would, in fact, pull her down further and confirm her doubts about herself. By carefully labelling her feelings, her parents would realise that what she needed was understanding and encouragement to believe that the effort she was making was indeed worthwhile.

It is important that the exercise of labelling is done thoroughly otherwise the whole process becomes vague and woolly; as a result it is less effective and open to misinterpretation. The difference between feelings is quite subtle and labelling helps clarity. For example being 'cross', 'angry', 'resentful', 'hurt' or 'frustrated' all have their special meanings, as do feeling 'fearful', 'anxious', 'worried' or 'concerned'. It is a case of the nearer one can get to the truth, the better the result.

The Problem Of Disguised Feelings

When a person's feelings are obvious but exaggerated and out of character, they are often a mask hiding the truth. They are a disguise, covering up the real feelings that lie beneath. Why is disguise necessary? The reason is that we all like to have a satisfactory picture of ourselves. If we do something which spoils this picture, then we may go to any length to deny it and so keep our self-image intact. In such circumstances not only do we deny to ourselves the true feelings of which we are ashamed, we also deny them outwardly to others.

Does this really matter? Yes, it often does, because if for any reason we have to face the truth, then our self-esteem will get an even worse knock than if we had faced up to the truth in the first place. An example will clarify this: Kevin's father was an excellent sportsman and Kevin desperately wanted to please him by being good at games. Unfortunately, Kevin had no sports talent at all. He felt very ashamed and could not come to terms with it. He got round it by pretending he was a great athlete and absented himself at games-time, but shot a big line at home about his prowess. He spent hours in a dream-world imagining himself in this role. His boasting was not just a lie, it was his way of keeping up the picture he wanted of himself. The trouble was that the boasting was out of character and this did not escape the notice of his parents. When they finally discovered the truth, their disgust at the pretence hit Kevin's pride harder than if he had faced the true facts and found out if his father's expectations were really as high as he feared.

If we are to be able to recognise and uncover disguises, then we must be on the lookout for unnatural or exaggerated feelings and we need to know all the forms disguises can take.

Shakespeare saw through one disguise when he wrote: "The lady doth protest too much, methinks". This is one of six main ways in which feelings of shame, guilt, disappointment, anger, hurt or fear may be disguised. The first way is to show exactly the opposite feeling to the one really being felt. For example: Amy poured out love, concern and attention on her new baby sister. She cried if she was not allowed to be with her all the time. Her interest was natural but her concern was far too exaggerated to be natural. She was disguising both fear and dislike of her new rival. The strength of her dislike made her feel deeply ashamed and she was fearful that she would express it by hurting the baby. She knew this would earn her mother's disapproval and she feared she might lose her mother's love. In fact her mother saw only the great affection displayed (the opposite of Amy's true feelings) and she mistakenly applauded it as admirable.

The second type of disguise shows itself in an escape into daydreams. There is no harm in daydreams; they can act as a spur to making the extra effort needed to reach a goal; but if they take over completely they sap energy and destroy concentration. They isolate a child from reality as the following example shows:

Paula, an only child, refused to play with other children who demanded give-and-take. She preferred to isolate herself in her dream-world where she could always do exactly as she wanted. As a result she made no friends and built her self-image up to unrealistic heights. Paula was hiding her fear of living life together with other children and having to compete with them in reality.

The third disguise takes the form of making someone else responsible for what "I" am feeling. For example, Janet claims that her teacher says that her best friend, Mary, is a real show-off who fancies herself too much. In fact this is how Janet feels about Mary but uses the disguise to hide her jealousy of which she is ashamed.

A fourth disguise takes the form of finding excuses: "I can't read well because the teacher never helps me. She only helps the others". This child is not facing up to the fact that she cannot keep up with the rest of her group. We all try to justify our actions and often make excuses for them instead of facing the true reason and doing something about it.

A fifth disguise takes the form of substituting the real target for hostile feelings by a false, often less dangerous, one. "I can't hit my sister, I will get into trouble if I do that so I will kick the furniture or the cat instead", or perhaps, "It's terrible to hate my mother so I'll hate my teacher instead. No one minds that". This may be true but her school work may suffer as a result!

Some people may even use themselves as the substitute target. They may keep hurting themselves instead of the person they really want to hurt. People in authority, the old and weak, even complete strangers may also be used as decoy targets. It becomes clear how the police can become a decoy for strong feelings against parents or loss of self-esteem due to boredom or unemployment.

The sixth disguise is a complicated one and often difficult to unravel. In this form, not only is the target for hostile feelings changed, but the feelings themselves are expressed by quite unconnected and irrational behaviour. For example, a child may not be able to face his aggressive feelings towards his parents for fear of not being loved. So he converts them into such irrational behaviour as a stutter, bed-wetting, nightmares, stealing, fear of the dark and so on. The substitution is quite unconscious; it happens automatically and is a safety-valve to preserve love and self-esteem. Such irrational behaviour is always a cry for help.

Another common form of this type of double substitution is when unacceptable feelings come to be expressed as the physical symptoms of illness. This sort of substitution is not difficult to understand when the close connection between feelings and physical effects is accepted. When people feel embarrassed or guilty, blood may rush to their face, they blush. Anger and indigestion are close partners, as are anxiety and headaches. Revulsion can cause a man to vomit, faint or wet his pants. It is not surprising that hurtful feelings can get converted into illness which a doctor will say has no physical basis. The pain felt is real, breathing may be difficult, appetite may be lost, rashes may appear and the bladder or bowels become uncontrollable. These or any other similar symptoms cannot be dismissed as malingering as they feel just as real as the symptoms of any purely physical complaint.

All these disguises, if causing concern, are best exposed. The uncomfortable feelings that attack self-esteem need to be discussed and the much-needed reassurance given. Feelings of failure, rejection, hate, anger, fear, jealousy and shame are the ones that most often hurt self-esteem. So these are the feelings that commonly become disguised. The reasons for these feelings are often out of all proportion to reality and if they can be faced as soon as they arise, a new confidence becomes evident and disguise is no longer necessary.

Some disguised feelings continue into adulthood and show themselves in the form of irrational fears, prejudices, and troublesome habits, all of which are difficult to break. If these symptoms cause concern, mean loss of livelihood or bring unhappiness then expert help will be needed to unravel the disguise. But trouble, time and expense can be saved by spotting these disguises when they first arise in the early years.

Children's Feelings Sometimes Differ From Those Of Adults

Even after parents have jumped the hurdle of recognising and unravelling disguised feelings, they have another concept to master before they can become fully competent in focusing on children's feelings. They need to learn that a child feels differently from adults. Most adults can put themselves in another adult's shoes. They simply ask themselves how they might feel in similar circumstances. It is much more difficult to change places with a child. The clues needed to make this jump can come from watching a child play and from listening to his conversation.

Once parents realise how much they can learn from this WATCHING and LISTENING, they will find the time to do so. By reading on, parents may become more aware of the differences in feelings between children and adults and so avoid an unwitting increase of anxiety and tension in their children.

The Fear Of Being Abandoned Or Rejected

Although parents may feel their children are well-cared for and loved, they should not ignore the possibility that these same children may still come to feel the fear of rejection if they are troublesome. Such threats as "Come at once or I will leave you here by yourself" or "Mummy doesn't love children who behave badly" stir up far more anxiety than is usually imagined. Situations quite out of parents' control can reinforce this fear in young children. Long, enforced separation, a death, stories of lost or forsaken children, all play their part. Perhaps more than anything, thoughtless comments made in moments of annoyance take a heavy toll: "You'll drive me crazy and then who will look after you?", or "A policeman will be after you if you don't stop crying. He will take you away. So watch it".

In a social club, a mother watching a game of tennis became impatient with her youngster who kept falling off her bike. She was heard to say, "I don't know how I put up with you". She then took a cursory look at the child's grazed knee, commenting "You'll live, unfortunately". The girl burst into tears and was far more than just crestfallen. Her worst fears about being rejected were confirmed. To make matters worse, the onlookers laughed at her mother's quip. The child was convinced that she was the target for everyone's ridicule.

Stories passed on by other children about quarrelling, beatings and even murder are not as uncommon as people think. The young cannot be screened from life. They have to live with it, not hide from it. Clinging, shyness, whining and crying, fear of going to sleep, bad dreams, fear of the dark, fear of never waking up (or fear that when they do, they will be all alone) are prevalent in children exposed to television violence. Fears of rejection are especially common between the ages of 2 and 4. Precautions to counteract these fears are easy to take. They consist of reassurance of being loved no matter what. Words that give a sense of togetherness, expressions that convince a child that his parents feel privileged to have him as part of the family add to the reassurance he may so badly need. Above all, happy bedtimes and separations made free from any traumatic anxiety, help to build up confidence and a sense of security.

Wishful Thinking

The feeling of responsibility and guilt over someone dying stems from another facet of the ways in which children think. They believe that wishes are all powerful. To an adult it is utterly preposterous that a child can feel responsible for, say his brother's or even his pet's death. To a child, his occasional wishes that he did not have a brother or could maltreat his pet, born perhaps of guilt, envy or jealousy, appear as reason enough to feel responsible. Wishful thinking is an everyday occurrence for a child. If by chance hostile wishes do come true, then a strong feeling of guilt is aroused. A wish such as "I hate you and hope you won't be happy", which by coincidence is followed by illness, hurt or absence of the person out of favour, will bring on a feeling of acute anxiety. For example: Chris, aged 10, envied his younger brother's ability at sport. On the day before the sports he did some wishful thinking. "Wouldn't it be great if Phil broke his leg." Later the same day Phil fell off a ladder and broke his arm and although Chris was nowhere near at the time, when he heard about the accident he was very upset and shut himself in his room. When at last his parents got him to open the door, they found that he had gouged a hole in his most treasured football. Chris himself could not explain why, but in fact he had punished himself for what he was convinced he had done to his brother. Wishful thinking can also make a muddle of truth and fiction. Wishes can readily be converted into facts.

"David gave me his animal book for keeps." This statement was hotly denied by a furious David who said that he had only lent the book for a short time.

"Mrs Brown said I could pick her apples", said Emily with a full basket of apples over her arm. Mrs Brown had merely said she could help pick the apples if she was invited. Emily was highly indignant when accused of stealing.

Jane, aged 14, while on holiday, rushed to her mother, tears much in evidence. "A man chased me and tried to push me over." Her fantasy had been so vivid that to her it was real although no such thing had happened. People had seen her in the village shop alone. Her somewhat inhibited family constantly warned about speaking to strange men but never discussed why. Questions on sex were never answered and maybe her story was her way of telling them that she wished for more open talk on the subject because it terrified her.

Ideas And Fears About Sex

Although this is a permissive age where sex is talked about quite freely, parents often impose a sense of guilt on their children by giving them mistaken ideas about their bodily functions. As mentioned in an earlier chapter, before adult ideas on personal hygiene are absorbed a child feels that everything about his body is precious, clean and interesting. When Liz, a toddler, gave Grandpa a present of a full potty, his "Ugh! Take it away, it stinks" brought tears of mortification and confusion. After all it was a special present and, in Liz's eyes, an achievement.

Although social custom is eventually accepted, parents need to avoid, in the process of teaching, making the child feel that what he produces is bad or disgusting.

Boys love to stand and produce a big stream. Girls watch their brothers and try to copy them. Inevitably they wonder, "Why haven't I got a proper spout?". What some parents do not know is that the small girl is not asking for anatomical facts alone, but fears that she has lost her spout or worse still, that it has been taken away because she is naughty. The fact that Mum is just like her does not answer her query or anxiety. Only understanding how she feels about it will produce the reassurance she needs. A boy, too, on seeing his sister or mother may wonder if he might lose his penis if he is naughty. If these fears are not going to arouse guilt then parents have to accept them and avoid calling them nonsense or merely covering up with anatomical accuracy alone. Boys also worry about circumcision and come to many wrong conclusions why many other boys are different. It is important to deal with any irrational fears about being deprived or cut and to avoid vague threats about what will happen if children continue to handle their genitals. If parents are ready to listen, many of these mistaken fantasies are likely to come to light and can then be dealt with quite easily.

Children have some weird ideas about babies. A mother may tell her child about where and how a baby grows, but it is often the questions that are never answered that breed anxiety. These include whether the baby comes out from Mummy's tummy button or from behind? Does Mum split open? Does she get hurt, is it dangerous, is there a lot of blood? These are the sorts of fears that add to the worry when Mother goes to hospital to have the baby.

Later, talk with other children often gives rise to a host of mistaken ideas: "Mum and Dad drink each other's wee!". Watching intercourse also provokes anxiety, and judging from the comments made by many 5 to 6 year olds, their interpretation is, to say the least, very bizarre. For example: "I've

76

seen my Dad try to kill my Mum. They fight in bed and Mum groans. It's awful my Dad is so cruel". In the context of understanding how a child feels about such things it is important to be able to equate sex with loving and give reassurance before there is any cause for worry. Naturally, watching intercourse is best avoided!

Parents so often put off talking frankly to their children about sex. It is so easy for children to absorb their parent's 'hang-ups' and to avoid this it helps to be aware of the urgency of dealing with fear or shame that may be distorting their ideas.

Showing Opposite Feelings At The Same Time

Children have the ability, to a much greater extent than adults, to express two different feelings about someone or something at the same time. Love and hate can be voiced with conviction within a few minutes. For example, negative statements such as "I hate you" or "I wish I never belonged to this family" may disturb some parents who do not realise that the same child may be voicing love and caring within the hour.

It is only when a child feels that it is safe to express negative as well as positive feelings, that he will adopt the healthy course of freely expressing his temporary aggression. His mixed-up emotions will come out only when he is assured that there is nothing strange or terrible about them. A person who can express only his lovable side may well be bottling up, and escaping from, the opposite aspects.

The older a child becomes, the more control he learns, and this control comes easily when it does not spring from fear. Understanding the fleeting nature of children's love, hate, joy and sadness, helps parents to see things in proportion and encourages them to let strong language flow over their heads. A sudden flare-up need not be taken too seriously or personally and knowing this, the temptation to retaliate can be resisted more easily.

The Tit For Tat Fears

Lastly, every child fears that if he is thinking, feeling or doing wrong, his parents will retaliate. It is as if he reasons like this: "If I hit you, you will hit me. You are bigger and stronger than me so I am bound to get the worst of it". Because he thinks like this, playing tit-for-tat with children is unwise as it reinforces this fear. If a young child is allowed to kick, bite or physically hurt his parents it will build up a fear of retaliation. A child needs to be restrained firmly but gently.

Children are often heard to say "I think you are unfair. You are cruel and I hate you", and then after a pause: "I suppose you don't like me now?". Their tone of voice may sound aggressive but an expression of anxiety often shows on their faces. In most cases anger disperses quite quickly and confidence replaces fear when reassurance is given that there will be no retaliation.

"You feel cross with me now, but even if I don't like the way you are behaving I still love you." The child's immediate reaction to this may be a vehement denial: "It's not true. I don't believe you. You don't love me. I hate you". This is simply asking for yet more reassurance and when this is repeated again and again the child's relief is obvious.

It is quite common for children to wish fleetingly that the people they love most, will die. They may fantasise about being adopted by other parents, kinder and richer than their own. Even such random daydreams sometimes bring a fear that something dreadful might really happen to pay them out for their wicked thoughts.

The intensity of these fears of retaliation can often be seen in play. A child who has misbehaved plays the part of a vindictive mother who doles out vengeance on the scale of the most wicked of witches in any fairy tale! A knowledge of how real this fear can be should warn adults about the necessity of avoiding anything that might reinforce it. The following examples show how easily this reinforcement can happen: "Now my lad, you kick me and you'll find that you will get one back that will send you to kingdom come".

"You play awkward with me and you will be surprised what will happen to you."

"You hit Bill and I'll hit you. That will teach you what it feels like."

Trying to be patient and restraining the temptation to hit back is not easy. However, even when patience is being tried to the limit, it may help to think: "Hold on. This is happening now but it will soon pass. My child will be showing his more loving, cooperative side if only I can keep my cool and stop myself from shouting back".

Helping Children Handle Their Uncomfortable Feelings

The final way to help ourselves focus on the feelings of our children lies in helping them to handle their strong and uncomfortable emotions. We need to give this important task at least the same priority as we give to training them in manners or teaching them how to cross a busy street safely. The mere acceptance of this responsibility will force us to be more aware and conscious of the quite complex feelings of our children. To be successful in helping our children in this way, we will need to recognise more clearly the situations that trigger off these strong feelings. This, in turn, will help us make more accurate guesses as to the cause of any upset and once this is known it is much easier to handle and deal with it. At this stage, parents might well suggest, "I can see clearly how helping my child handle his feelings will help me focus on them but I have no idea how to set about giving this help. What do I have to do?". What follows may go some way to answering this question.

Strong feelings create great tension and the most effective way to help children handle them is to allow and encourage them to release this tension in as many harmless ways as possible. The ways to do this will be dealt with in detail in Chapter 11.

One of these ways is worth special mention here. The most natural way of allowing a child to let off steam is to allow him to express his strong feelings: "I feel mad", "I hate you", "I would like to smash you to bits" are typical examples. This abusive language is sometimes hard to accept without showing disapproval, but it is vitally important to allow children's angry words, however strong, to flow over our heads without challenging or disputing them. Not only does this bring great relief to the child but the words replace physical attack or worse behaviour. A child's fantasies, whilst he is in a rage, can also be allowed full verbal rein, however horrific they may be.

There are a number of other ways to lessen the intensity of a child's feelings in a moment of stress and in the quieter times to follow. One of these is to bring home to the child that having strong feelings is natural to us all. The more insecure a child feels the more he will tend to be overwhelmed by emotion. Reassurance that everyone experiences uncomfortable feelings at one time or another will reduce this insecurity.

This insecurity, born of his strong feelings, can also be reduced by talking to him about our own difficulties. Our own acceptance of our bad tempers and black moods is most clearly shown by being able to discuss them openly. It is, therefore, sensible to talk to our children and bring home to them through our personal experience that excusing or denying strong feelings does not bring any long term relief.

Another way we can help is by good example. If we face a fear-provoking situation clamly then our calm will be infectious. If on the other hand we panic then our fear is sure to catch on. The same applies to the way we handle our exasperation, resentment and hurt in front of our children.

A child's feelings are always intensified if they are coupled with guilt. He will become even more frightened and resentful if, in a crisis, he is made to feel guilty. Obviously, then, guilt needs to be kept to a minimum at times of stress. Guilt often arises when strong feelings trigger off behaviour that the child regrets and which earns the obvious disapproval of those he loves. Behaviour that lowers self-esteem and clashes with a child's conscience will also be guilt-provoking. Parents can help by avoiding disapproval in times of stress, directing this disapproval at the behaviour, not the child. For example, it is better in a moment of exasperation to say, "Being interrupted all the time is annoying and does not make me want to listen to you", rather than "You are a very rude child. Stop interrupting me!". Guilt can be further reduced if the subjects which tend to arouse it are discussed openly and are fully understood.

Parents can also bring comfort by staying close when a child is in an uncontrollable tantrum and so be there to prevent his doing anything destructive or harmful. The child may protest at any restraint at the time, but inwardly, he will be grateful and much relieved. In this context it has already been explained that a young child should never be allowed to make a physical attack on his parents or others on whom he depends for love. If unrestrained, such attacks usually produce strong feelings of guilt as their aftermath.

Fantasies lose their sense of danger if they are brought out into the open and reassurance given. Being sure that God and secular authority are helpful rather than punitive will also save a child from building up feelings of guilt and fear.

Finally, the knowledge that forgiveness is possible and that making amends is acceptable, goes a long way to relieve guilt. Bouts of anger and resentment usually fade quite quickly if they are expressed in some harmless way, such as stamping a foot, kicking a ball or using strong words. Great patience and forbearance is required to ride out a storm. The time taken is always shortened if we focus on the feelings and give every chance for tension to be released. These moments of stress can also be used as opportunities to try out one of the most successful of the tension-releasing skills, Responsive Listening. This is dealt with in the next chapter.

CHAPTER 10 : Releasing Tension By Using Responsive Listening

The Difference Between Just Hearing And Really Listening

Hearing is a simple matter of using one of our senses. Sounds are transmitted and their logical sequence makes sense and in this way information is passed from one person to another. When the word listening is used in this chapter it is used to convey much more than just hearing. It is intended to imply a full awareness of, and concern for, the person speaking. In the case of parents listening to their children, they should try to convey the message: "We hear you. We care about you and what you are feeling, as well as what you are saying".

"Responsive Listening" goes even further. Responses made while listening need to show a willingness to hear more and to encourage continuing communication. So when people listen responsively they do not use only their ears and voice: their whole body is involved. Their eyes express their attention and concern, they stop what they are doing and perhaps move closer to the speaker. With a small child, they may stoop or kneel so as to be at the same level and maybe touch an arm or hand to show understanding.

This is the opposite from what often takes place. There is a readiness to interrupt, our impatience shows through by the tapping of a foot, the drumming of fingers or finishing off a sentence, even answering before the child has finished speaking. We often give the impression that what WE have to say is all that really matters and the quicker the conversation is over, the better. This is no way to release tension!

Responsive Listening is nothing new. It is a well-tried method used by doctors, teachers, counsellors, therapists, social workers and personnel officers. Anyone seeking help over a problem needs to be encouraged to talk about it, to examine his own motives and to express his needs. Confidence in the listener is imperative before feelings will be openly expressed. There has to be the certainty that the listener will not judge, criticise or try to impose his own opinions or solutions. In the case of children appealing for help, they want to feel accepted persons in their own right. Whenever a conflict develops at home, or when a child has a particular problem, then the skill of responsive listening can be used to advantage. It can play a vital part when communication is breaking down and tension is mounting.

How To Show Awareness And Encourage Communication

An atmosphere of friendly, uncritical acceptance of views and feelings will invite a child to talk. Once there is a lack of understanding, opposition or judgment, then the tendency will be to clam up, rebel and feel even more frustration. Two examples may help to illustrate this:

Lucy complains to her parents: "I feel so unattractive. It's miserable". Her parents might respond with: "Oh, what nonsense, Lucy. You look fine.

Anyway, it's character that counts, not looks. Cheer up". This reply will probably drive Lucy into angry silence or an argumentative outburst. Her parents, meaning to be kind, have completely failed to show the understanding she wants and have closed the door on the opportunity to go on talking about what is bothering her. This could be her general lack of popularity. A better reply would have been: "Poor you. I can see you feel miserable. Anything special got you down?". Lucy will now sense that her feelings have been accepted. She will also hear sympathy and a willingness to listen to more. She is encouraged to go on talking. Her real problem will now be brought out into the open and it is hoped dealt with.

The other example is one that every family will recognise. While out walking with mother, a child falls, starts crying and will not continue. The conversation may go on like this: "Come on, what's the matter?". The child responds, "My knee hurts. I can't walk properly". Mother glances down and decides there is little amiss and says, "Oh, rubbish! You can walk perfectly well. It's nothing, only a little graze. It can't hurt much and anyway you are far too old to fuss over a small thing like that". The child becomes angry. He thinks, "Mother does not care or understand. It is my knee and I know it hurts. What right has she to say it doesn't?". His feelings are denied, which calls for making more fuss over his knee. Even if subdued into silence, his hostility will not disappear.

How much better had Mother said, "Oh poor you, let me see. You say it hurts. I do hope it is better soon". Reassured that Mother cares, there is a good chance that in a moment he will drop the whole thing and relationships with Mother will remain warm.

In these two examples, a slight difference in the slant of what is said can alter the child's response dramatically. Cooperation can be easily encouraged rather than brought to a full stop.

To reiterate, in making the correct response in moments of stress, the parent needs to show that he is listening, is trying to understand and is ready to see the child's angle, even if he disagrees. He needs to show that he wants the child to talk about his problem until it is clear. Adult opinions are best kept to oneself, criticism checked and any approval or disapproval avoided. Instead, acknowledgement of how the child feels or sees his problem and encouragement to find his own solution, will stabilise the situation.

To make a successful response of this kind, the listener needs to be in a receptive mood. If he is not, it will show in his expression and tone of voice. Active interest, full attention and willingness to spare the time to listen are essentail factors.

Receptive attitudes, bred of real concern, can easily be recognised. For instance, if someone says, "I can't find my specs. I need them urgently", then any response such as "That's tough" or "Bad luck" can, depending on tone or emphasis, either mean "So what? You are always looking for them" or "I'm very concerned for you". The simplest way to show concern is by using words and a tone that are in themselves an invitation to continue talking. They also need to reduce any fear over being made to look a fool and instead, aim at preserving self-respect.

Different Types Of Response

When a listening parent says as little as possible, it opens the door for the child to do the talking. In fact, receptive listening often calls for a minimum response, just enough to show continued attention. Voiced with concern, such phrases as, "Oh, I see", "Mmmm", "And so?", "Yes?", may be particularly useful when the real nature of the problem is not clear and more clues are wanted from further conversation. The child may merely need a verbal prod to continue talking. Just a grunt may be enough when listening to a minor problem. These first minimal responses sometimes need to be followed up by more obvious evidence of understanding. Phrases can be used such as, "Really? Is that so?"; "Who'd have thought that"; "Well, how about that. Tell me more"; "I'm all ears" or "Sounds as if this matters to you".

There are times when even more encouragement may be needed to start a reluctant child talking: "Would it help to discuss it?" or "Would you like to tell me how you feel about it?". The decision to confide or not is up to the child; the parent's role remains that of a willing and receptive listener. The types of phrases already mentioned, emphasise this role and as they are commonly used in everyday conversation, they should come easily.

There is, however, a slightly less usual way to build up a child's confidence to continue talking. The parent needs to prove to the child that he is trying to understand the situation and that he is grasping the true feelings being expressed. This reassurance can be given by REFLECTING BACK to the speaker the feelings that lie behind what he has said. The words need to act as a mirror so that there is a certainty in the child's mind that an attempt is being made to understand. It must be made clear that reflecting a child's statement is not a parrot-like repetition of his words. For example, if he says, "I don't want to have Mr Smith as my teacher", the parrot response would be, "You feel you do not want Mr Smith as your teacher?". With justification he might well retort, "That's what I said. Weren't you listening?". On the other hand if Mother replied: "You seem not to like Mr Smith teaching you", it would be a true reflective response. It shows an attempt to understand why he does not want Mr Smith as a teacher and so encourages him to elaborate and contradict it if the guess is wrong.

Further examples may help to clarify this point, which at first can be confusing: Chris, aged 7, shows signs of unusual agitation, clings to his Mother and says: "I wish Dad didn't have to go away to this conference. I shall miss him so much".

Father is often away and this has never produced this sort of reaction before. Mother senses there is more here than meets the eye and tries a reflec-

83

tive response in order to hear more. "You feel sad because Dad is away?" Chris knows that Mum is at least trying to understand even though she has got it wrong. He is sufficiently encouraged to continue: "Well, things can go wrong with aeroplanes". Mum, not knowing this is a red herring, tries again with a straight reflection.

"It's worrying to think about accidents happening." This is enough to keep the ball rolling.

"Oh, I don't suppose accidents often happen. I wonder what Dad is thinking about?" Ah! Is this a possible clue?

"You feel Dad is concerned about something?"

"Well, he didn't give me the usual hug when he left." A positive reply at last. Mother tries again: "You feel he was cross with you?". Each reflection leads the direction of the talk back to the child and every new angle that comes up can be mirrored back to show that it is understood. It often takes time and patience for the point to be reached where the child's confidence is sufficiently built up for him to express his fears. Finally Chris says, "He wasn't cross, but I know he wanted to take his pen-knife and he couldn't find it".

"You feel he might blame you?" It is a guess which strikes home.

"Oh Mum, I only borrowed it. I didn't mean to keep it" and Chris produces the knife from his pocket. Mother avoids criticism: "Perhaps you wished you had one just the same?".

"I'll put it back on Dad's desk." Chris has found his own solution. The whole incident may seem to be time-consuming but how much better to resolve a problem with relationships still warm, rather than save a bit of time and leave Chris's guilt to fester.

Often when children quarrel, it helps to reflect what they feel about the situation. A child may say in anger, "I hate Sally. She's a show-off". The response might be, "Showing off is something you dislike. It annoys you?" A simple reflective phrase like this helps to take the sting out of her anger. There is relief at being understood, not contradicted. A final example follows:

MARK: "I didn't take two biscuits. I tell you I didn't."

MOTHER: "You are trying to convince me that you didn't take two biscuits."

MARK: "Look in my mouth. You see there is only one."

MOTHER: "You want me to believe you only had one?"

MARK: "Well, I didn't take two together."

MOTHER: "You were wondering if I would be cross?"

MARK: "You would be, wouldn't you?"

MOTHER: "I said one was your share for tea."

MARK: "Well, OK, I will do without one tomorrow."

It is easy to imagine how accusations could have started up a feeling of resentment in Mark. Instead, his lie and disobedience were solved and the solution produced by the child himself. His knowledge of what was right and fair came to the top because he was not forced into a position of self-defence.

Using reflective phrases is useful when tempers are aroused, when indignation flares up or when guilt, fear and insecurity are in evidence. Not only does this type of response cool the situation but in the end it encourages co-operation. Sometimes a child shows a wish to confide but finds it difficult to get started. Then, if the parent has no idea where the problem lies, repeated reflective responses may tend to make the conversation go round and round, getting nowhere. This non-productive cycle can best be broken by the parent taking a tentative guess and putting this guess to the test. He may put his suggestion and then add "Is that what you mean?". If the answer is yes then the child can be invited to continue. If the answer is no, then another guess can be offered. For example: Sean snatches a toy away from a visiting friend and a fight ensues. Mother has no idea as to the root cause of Sean's action. She separates them and then has her first guess:

MOTHER: "You want to stop Jim playing with your train?"
SEAN: "He can't have it. So there!"
MOTHER: "Perhaps he has had his turn with it?"
SEAN: "Yes. He can't have it any more."
MOTHER: "Do you think he will break it?"
SEAN: "No, he won't."
MOTHER: "Maybe you feel a bit cross because I was playing with him for quite a while?"
SEAN: "You always make a fuss of visitors."
MOTHER: "Do you feel this is very unfair?"
SEAN: "Of course it's unfair."

The real cause for resentment has come to light, but only after several reflective guesses had been made and rejected. Once Sean realised that his point of view was understood, the need to resist was thrust aside, now no longer a bone of contention. Feelings of jealousy are often carefully hidden and can be brought out into the open only when encouragement is given.

MOTHER: "You often feel that I am unfair to you?"
SEAN: "Well, you often stick up for other people against me."
MOTHER: "It must be wretched feeling like that."
SEAN: "Well, I just wish I was the only one. Then you would love me best, all of the time."

This short, trivial conversation brought Sean's feelings of jealousy out into the open. The message got through to his mother and she realised she must make sure he feels he has his fair share of attention and love.

Considering the following questions may help parents begin to make reflective responses, by focusing their attention on the right words to use and attitudes to adopt:

1) Am I showing care by using my eyes, hands, voice and expression in a sympathetic way?
2) Do I stop what I am doing and really listen when there is a problem?
3) What feeling is my child trying to express?
4) What message is he trying to give me?
5) When I make a response is it inviting him to go on talking?
6) Do I show him clearly I am trying to understand?
7) Do I keep my opinions and solutions to myself?
8) Do I give him a chance to lessen the tension he is feeling?
9) Am I helping him to find his own way through his problems?
10) Are there any clues I can gather from his behaviour?

The Difficulties Of Learning This New Skill

Finding clues to help understanding

The last question, "Are there any clues I can gather from observing my child's behaviour?" highlights one of the real difficulties in using Responsive Listening. This problem arises when we just do not know what has triggered off the trouble or what are the precise feelings aroused.

As already mentioned, when faced with this situation we have to make a guess or series of guesses until we hit the nail on the head. The ability to guess near the mark not only enriches the quality of responsive listening but also saves a lot of time! What then can we do to improve our guessing skill and insight?

The best way to learn how our children tick is through watching, listening, talking and paying attention to their play, their rivalries and emotional reactions. We are apt to think that this understanding will be absorbed through the skin without any effort. This can be true in a close-knit family, but when time is limited and life busy, we can find ourselves horribly out of touch.

A definite effort needs to be made to spend time alone with children, talking and playing as well as keeping an ear open to what often seems inconsequential chatter. The amount of information that is waiting to be picked up in this way has to be experienced to be believed! One mother was very sceptical about watching and listening while her child was playing. She told her story this way:

"If kids are quiet, I thank my stars and leave them alone. Yesterday however, I gained some valuable insight in an unexpected way. Lunch had been the usual battle. Betsy toyed with her food, spilt it, spat it out and I became so exasperated I shouted at her. She put her tongue out at me, went sullen and ate nothing more. That evening I heard her chatting to her toy fish while in her bath. It took me by surprise to hear her mimicking my voice in this way: 'Have you washed your hands? Don't slouch, sit up straight, don't talk with your mouth full. Hold your knife properly — eat slowly — stop fidgeting – look at that mess – it's revolting to spit things out. No sweets until you finish your firsts . . .'. Her voice was bossy and petulant. She made me sound very unreasonable. Suddenly I realised that all my nagging was taking the joy out of meal-times and certainly not teaching good table manners. I decided there and then that I must avoid being so fussy and not be put on the defensive. Eating was going to be Betsy's responsibility and manners something she would have to pick up by amicable discussion and example." This mother gained valuable insight into a never-ending problem through listening to her child at play.

The next example concerns an older child. Adam's father admitted that he usually tried to close his ears to his children's idle chatter and get on with whatever he was doing. He came to admit that this was a mistake after an incident in the home. His daughter had watched Adam grappling with his 'O' level maths homework and saw him crumple up one page after another and fling them on the floor. She commented: "You seem a bit upset this evening" and he replied: "Well, what do you expect? There is no one to help me and anyway I don't see the point of it all. Where is it going to get me?".

Adam's father was reading the newspaper but this time he happened to hear and register the exchange. He suddenly realised that he was in a position to give the help that was needed. As long as there were no complaints or bad reports he had not interfered with Adam's schooling and he had not discussed his son's future as it all seemed too bleak for not-so-bright school leavers. It came to him in a flash of insight, triggered by the brief comments he had heard, that these were just excuses for his lack of awareness. He wondered how many similar indirect pleas for help and support he had failed to notice simply because he never bothered to listen unless Adam approached him directly.

Responsive Listening can sound unnatural

Parents who are new to the idea of Responsive Listening often complain . . . "It sounds so silly, so trite" . . . or "The family will think I've gone crazy if I start talking like that. It sounds so mechanical and unnatural".

It is perfectly true that at first reflective responses do sound strange. A professional counsellor who uses this technique takes many years to train, so a parent should not be surprised that perfecting the skill takes patience just as any skill does. First attempts once made, when a stressful situation presents itself, are likely to bring more confidence and this makes the effort to continue practising the skill seem worthwhile.

The fear of the mechanical, parrot-like effect has already been mentioned. If the response does sound like this then it is wrong. Responsive Listening entails hearing the innuendo, gaining clues, interpreting feelings and then reflecting this understanding in the right way. All this requires active thought; no mere mechanical process here!

87

Children who have been used to being bombarded by their parents opinions, who have been criticised and rebuked and had ready-made solution forced on them, will certainly find the new response very strange indeed. I may come as a shock. They cannot help but notice it and certainly may won der what has come over their parents.

It is best for parents to bring the whole idea into the open and discus the new approach to relationships with their children. After all it is not a secret weapon but something that will benefit both adult and child alike There is often good-tempered banter and some leg-pulling from older childrer at first, but the idea is soon accepted and welcomed. The subject can b approached like this:

"Don't be too surprised if things are a bit different around here. I feel have found a new way to try to be more understanding of your point of view Perhaps if I listen a bit more, we will be able to sort things out better. Obvi ously it is fairer if everyone is given a chance to have his say without being interrupted by grown-ups giving their opinions and decisions."

Even teenagers, who may be suspicious of the first halting efforts, soor find they like being heard. Once communication becomes easier and more re laxed, there is no doubt that the young enjoy doing their share of talking, ex pressing opinions and feeling that responsibility for finding solutions rest with them unless they clearly ask for and welcome help.

Some fears about Responsive Listening

Families often start out bravely practising the new skill when tensior rises, and then their courage fails them and they ask "Isn't it too permissive won't things get out of hand, won't children take a reflection as tantamount to agreement?".

These fears are groundless because the end result of Responsive Listen ing lies in finding a solution that is acceptable to all. This final solution, to be effective and long-lasting, has to meet both the adult's and the child's needs so there can be no question of giving way; rather it is creating a climate where mutually-agreed answers to problems become possible. When feelings have been expressed and tension lessened a child is usually much more cooperative to the extent that parents, recently started on responsive listening, have beer heard to comment in amazement, "I never knew kids could respond so differ ently in such a comparatively short time".

Some parents fear that when a child expresses opinions or values with which they disagree, then reflecting these feelings back to the child will only serve to reinforce them. On the contrary, this show of understanding by re flection will at least keep communication open and allow further amicable discussion during which parents can put across their views.

Many parents find it difficult to listen to opinions and values that differ from their own without immediately trying to intervene and correct the mis taken ideas. The temptation to teach, preach, dictate or persuade has to be withstood. This hangover of keeping all the power in adults' hands usually backfires. It may work for a while but there comes a time when a child will revolt against too many imposed ideas. The danger is that in revolting, a child may go to the opposite extreme, making compromise more difficult, if not impossible. Passing on ideas and values has an important place in child-rearing but not at moments when tension is running high andcommunciation liable to break down.

An example of some parents' fear of egging on a child: Fred, aged 15, threw down his school bag and announced to his mother: "I'm not going to bother about going to school tomorrow. Plenty of boys don't, and no one finds out. We are not learning anything worthwhile". His mother's reflective reply could have been, "You feel that school is a waste of time?". But her fear that Fred would take this as some measure of acceptance of his attitude and so encourage truancy, prevented her from taking this positive step. She confided to a friend: "If I let that sort of thing go he might think that I go along with his truanting. He is in with a dreadful crowd. I can't help telling him how mistaken he is, how he is being led astray and how much he will reg-ret it later". She went on to tell of Fred's reaction to her homily, which was predictable: he turned on his heels, walked out, no doubt to join his unsuit-able friends. His sole comment was that she talked a load of crap.

Supposing his mother had had the courage to reflect Fred's feelings. Knowing how Fred felt about school could have led to something positive be-ing done about it. Instead, shortly after this incident, he was referred to an adolescent centre for school refusal. There it was found that he lacked any sense of achievement, had no ideas about his future and was heading fast to-wards vandalism and petty crime. Far more for his parents to fear than from listening to his outspoken point of view and thereby enlisting his cooperation to try and sort things out, before he found himself in trouble with the law.

Responsive Listening can fail

What happens when a child refuses to talk even when encouraged? This usually happens when advice, questioning, criticism and nagging have become a well-established pattern in the past. Older children especially can be suspi-cious of any sudden change in attitude towards them and may not respond to a frank admission of what lies behind a change. They may think it some sort of con, some way to catch them out. Some may defend themselves by asking endless questions and demanding opinions as if they have a fear of ever having to expose their own. Responsive Listening then leads nowhere and presents a problem that cannot be solved overnight. A fairly long-drawn out process of rebuilding mutual trust will have to be gone through and Responsive Listen-ing never forced on a child until he is in the mood to talk and confide. It is better to drop trying to communicate until he is ready.

89

This mutual trust is best built up by avoidance of the old critical attitude, by doing much more listening until the child shows the first signs of willingness to communicate. Only then can he be encouraged further by Responsive Listening.

This skill can also fail if a parent's motives in seeking a solution are suspect. Many an intelligent boy or girl will stubbornly resist any move towards solutions that smack of parents trying to suit themselves. Responsive Listening can then begin to sound like disguised interrogation or an attempt to win a child round by kindness. In such cases it simply increases irritation and distrust, and the skill, however correctly performed, will fail to produce results. For example, Neville's mother wanted to get him in a good mood because she needed help to bring in the coal from the garden shed. She started with a straightforward plea for help:

MOTHER: "I am so busy, please give me a hand with the coal."

NEVILLE: "I'm busy too, I can't do it now."

MOTHER: "You feel hassled?"

NEVILLE: "Stop bothering me."

MOTHER: "We all feel out of sorts at times." Neville suspects Mother's motives behind her sudden concern for his welfare and so turns the tables:

NEVILLE: "And you are furious because I won't fetch and bloody carry for you."

MOTHER: "You are a rude, selfish boy." Tension rises rapidly and cooperation falls to zero.

Making Responsive Listening succeed

The words to use, when to use them, and some of the common difficulties that can be encountered have all been mentioned. To be sure of success there has to be, in addition, a belief in fair play, a belief in the skill and a wish to make it work. There has to be a spirit of true compromise and finally acceptance of the fact that, given the chance, a child can find solutions to his own problems. Responsive Listening cannot be used to manipulate children to parents' advantage.

The following excerpt, taken out of a tape sent by a mother who had just started learning the skill of Responsive Listening, describes her experiences, her difficulties and eventual success:

"I have been looking forward to making this tape as it is two weeks since I started to try out Responsive Listening. I can't help smiling at the enjoyment I'm getting over talking away and knowing you will be listening! You see I really am convinced now that knowing one is being heard brings an odd sort of relief and certainly encourages me to let go and say what I really feel. Mind you, I'm not much good at it yet but I suppose it is early days.

Joyce (her 3 year old daughter) is already less of a pest, at least some of the time. Anyway I feel that I have something definite to work on and that terrible nagging fear that I would lose control and wallop her, has gone. Oh, I must tell you. When Peter (her husband) first heard the reflecting going on with Joyce, he said I sounded like a gramaphone with the needle stuck. Obviously I wasn't hitting the right, what you call accepting, sort of tone. I was more worried about the actual words and was tempted to just copy hers back. But I am getting better now and had a real good laugh when I tried it on Peter and it worked like a charm! With Joyce I'm still making mistakes. I'm so tempted to tell her to get up and go and play and stop pestering me. I must be honest. I've said all the wrong things but at least I have realised what I am doing and even managed to stop half way through a tirade. She has taken to Responsive Listening like a duck to water − I only half believed it would work − but the amazing thing is she is already less trouble to handle. She screams, kicks, tells me she hates me and I stop her just by saying 'You feel very cross with me' and far sooner than previously she quietens down and then hugs me to bits.

I actually got her dressed today without the usual struggle. At first she refused so I said, 'You don't want to put your clothes on − is that right?' Joyce still continued her usual tack: 'No I won't, no I won't'. I just repeated it again about her not wanting her clothes on. I was getting a bit desperate as this happened about three, or was it four times. All of a sudden, for no reason that I could understand, she got dressed with no more fuss. I think it was getting a rise out of me every day that made the confrontation almost a ritual. I still don't understand the reasons for her behaviour but please tell me if you think I am going along the right lines? One thing is for sure I am feeling better in myself . . . "

This is an encouraging story that is very common with parents who wholeheartedly try Responsive Listening for the first time when they are faced with more hassle than they can tolerate.

Unlike the mother who sent the last tape there may be parents who say they cannot get through to their children even when using Responsive Listening. One is bound to wonder if they are failing to use the technique correctly. Here are some typical responses mistakenly thought of as the proper use of the skill:

1) "Oh, what a shame!" This phrase is meant to show sympathy but is often taken as pity by an angry child. Unless used with care it can come over as insincere, especially if it is an habitual expression.

2) "I can quite understand how you feel about school but I am very SORRY FOR YOUR TEACHER." This comment is unwittingly going to the defence of the other person who is involved in the stress situation. It is only the child's point of view that matters at the critical moment when Responsive Listening is needed.

3) "YOU DON'T REALLY FEEL as cross as you say you are." This

attempted reassurance is an outright denial of the child's feelings and this is never helpful.

4) "IF I WERE YOU I would calm down before taking any decisions." This is uncalled-for advice and however sensible it is, ears are usually closed to it while tension is high.

5) "You call yourself a silly fool; so it seems you must feel a fool." Reflecting names that people call themselves should be avoided as it does nothing to build up their self-image. It may even seem to confirm the name-tag, which is seldom welcome. Being hard on oneself is very different from hearing someone else be the same, even if it is justified.

All the above are commonly-used responses made with the best intentions. They increase tension and discourage further conversation. Responsive Listening should aim at showing acceptance of a person as he is. We need to be aware that criticising a child in his hearing, forever fussing to improve his looks, putting his hair in order, improving his posture, all deny this acceptance even if the words used in Responsive Listening show understanding. In these cases actions speak louder than words.

When someone else accepts us as we are and accepts how we feel, then we relax. We find new courage to go on explaining our viewpoint and this in turn releases more tension. More on this theme follows in the next chapter.

CHAPTER 11 : Further Ways For Children To Release Tension

Short And Long Term Options

There is ample evidence that Responsive Listening invites further communication and warms relationships, but sometimes this is not enough to release all the tension that is there. A difficult environment, a family break-up and countless other factors of family life can keep stress up to a high level.

When a family appears to be relaxed, it probably means that they have discovered ways and means of channelling tension into satisfactory outlets. It is, therefore, worth identifying these outlets. They fall into two broad categories, one to be used when tension has reached the explosive stage and the other for use in times of quiet when all seems to be plain sailing.

They are, in effect, short and long term options. By short term is meant those used during sudden crises, when emotional pressures are high and immediate release is needed to avoid an explosion. This is the old safety-valve idea. By long term is meant the action taken when there is no special tension but surplus underlying stress needs a continuous outlet. Supplying these outlets is well within the capabilities of all families. In most cases, all that is called for is the supplying of opportunities and materials through which a child can find release from stress through his own activities.

The Safety Valve Of Words

The easiest and most obvious of the ways to let off steam is to let a person express his feelings in words. Parents need to allow their children to do this and to accept it without getting hot and bothered. A child may taunt, be rude or swear but in an explosive situation there is a need for him to express his feelings without disapproval.

Some parents may find this hard to take. It will help if from the start there are limits as to where, when and against whom these outbursts will be tolerated. Each family needs to decide how far it can allow this outlet to be used. Children quickly realise what is acceptable and will abide by it providing there is not complete prohibition on this kind of tension outlet. Generally parents agree that a verbal outlet directed at them in private is acceptable. An explosion directed at understanding parents is far safer than taking it out on brother or sister or people outside the family.

When discussing this problem of where to draw the line, a group of teenagers saw the snags and faced up to them. The following extracts were taken from a recording of their discussion.

"I'm lucky. If I let fly my parents can take it. Usually I am the one to apologise — but only when things have cooled down."

"It is safest to say exactly what one thinks only to one's folks. A friend is apt to hold it against you later."

"I like saying exactly what I feel but I don't think saying really cruel things is fair."

"I agree, I think one should avoid being cruel and I also think one should avoid letting go in public. It's somehow humiliating – not like at home."

"On the cruel thing – I also think it is mean to attack someone's really soft spot."

"But that's the whole point! When I feel really mad with someone going for their soft spot is a sure way of hitting back."

"Well, maybe so, but I don't think it's fair. We do it of course, but without realising how cruel it is."

"We've talked about this at home and there is general agreement on how we let off steam. Personal attacks isn't one of them, with us, anyway."

"We have rules at home too. My old man swears as good as it comes, so he doesn't turn a hair if I do. He won't stand for me calling Ma names, even in private."

It is clear that these boys and girls thought about the rules they made for themselves and although they all seem to be in favour of being able to express their thoughts and feelings freely, they were ready to draw some lines which they would not cross.

Parents can expect verbal attacks to differ according to the ages of the children. Between the ages of 2 and 4 they are full of dire threats such as: "I hate you, I'll cut up your dress, I'll bite you, I'll leave you all alone and never come back, I'll hit you so hard it will leave a big mark", or "I hope you die."

These childish wishes, so often reflecting the very things they fear may happen to them, can be taken lightly. It is helpful to show acceptance by simple reflection: "You feel cross with me". This takes the sting away and brings the added reassurance that, even if they are angry, they are still loved. Fear of retaliation is never far below the surface at this age so it is important that threats of hurting physically are firmly but gently restrained.

Between the ages of 5 and 10, the child's imagination is less vivid and often the attack is in the form of a general reproach:

"You are the worst mother ever."

"You are unfair. You give Jim more than me."

"You are mean. You never give me what I want, you only know how to nag."

From 10 to 16 years the type of expression becomes more scathing and critical:

"You don't know what 'cool' really means."

"You are the end as far as I am concerned. You'll never understand."

"Why don't you leave me alone? You are messing up my life."

Name-tags such as 'fool', 'bitch', 'bastard', and swearing may be the order of the day if they are commonly used in the home; if they are used only to shock, then reflection in paraphrase stops them becoming an issue when tension runs high. For instance, the reflection might go like this: "You feel very strongly about that", "You are trying to convince me", or, if it is the case, "You want me to say I am shocked".

Using Responsive Listening and showing understanding of the feelings being expressed, rather than concentrating on the hurtful words, is the parents' answer to tolerating a momentary outburst.

The Safety-Valve Of Actions

Another short-term pressure release is by action. We all know the relief that comes from stamping a foot or banging the table. A child, as well as an adult, should be allowed the luxury of working off his tension through actions that in themselves are harmless.

A child cannot be allowed to hurt people or damage property, however desirable it is for him to let off steam. Alternative harmless ways can usually be found by giving the opportunity for rowdy play. Too much encouragement to act aggressively is not wise as it can add to the tension, but if the child chooses his own play outlet with sand, water, kicking a ball or jumping up and down, then things usually calm down. The overwhelmingly angry feelings need the safety of an accepting adult's presence; one who will not retaliate but whom the child feels will stop him from doing anything bad.

A young child wants to hit his brother but his attention can be diverted to a doll that can be safely bashed or a sand castle that can be jumped on and demolished. This type of action is best suited to the 2 and 4 year group.

The older child soon learns to copy the adult forms of release. These, for the most part, are verbal, but the foot-stamping and door-slamming are soon copied. Diverting the actions of an older child may not be easy. The children themselves often find diversion by turning on the television, listening to pop music with high sound level, eating ravenously, playing darts or pretending no one exists at home but themselves!

When possible, by accepting their anger and keeping communication open, it is safer to encourage the child to stay at home while he works off his frustration. Once contact is lost, the chance of regaining cooperation is gone and with it any hope of finding a quick solution. Children of all ages, when very angry, will usually prefer to stay somewhere near an adult whom they know is understanding. The adult may not agree with the reasons for the anger but needs to accept the reality of how the child feels. This fact can be a help in dealing with teenagers to prevent them rushing off to seek revenge or add to the damage elsewhere.

Long-Term Methods Of Tension Release

Play provides the easiest and most effective way by which tension can be released in children up to 10 years old. This age is arbitrary and does depend to some extent on individual tastes, abilities and interests.

A list of the types of play materials which are best suited for this purpose may help parents. First there are the big outdoor and large playroom toys such as a punch-bag, something to climb, cushions or balls to kick, large skittles to knock down, sand to mess about in, bikes, toy cars, pretend boats, noisy toys such as drums, trumpets and cymbals, water and hose-pipe, tins, a place to call a house, toy guns, pistols, etcetera. A garden or yard is needed for most of these and if a child lives in a flat, then a playground may provide at least some of these kinds of material.

It is surprising how inventive a child can be, how much his imagination alone can supply, if materials of the sort described are hard to come by. So much stress can be released by playing at being Superman, a monster, an astronaut or just rushing around making a lot of noise. Challenging physical tasks can also help.

The indoor toys consist of old clothes to dress up in, a cosy place to make a house (even if only under a table), some soft cushions or a rag bag, dolls and other soft toys but especially, if at all possible, a set of miniature dolls, depicting Mum, Dad, Gran and Grandpa. Bricks and blocks are needed for building, some dough, clay or Plasticine, paint, large sheets of newspaper, blunt scissors, cups and something to pour from, the use of Mum's mincing machine, weighing scales and unbreakable bowls and wooden spoons. A sand-tray about 18 inches by 2 feet by 3 inches deep is a must. This can be used indoors and is the base for making model scenes. The bits for these scenes can be bought gradually, cut out or made.

For older children from 8 to 16 years, painting and making model scenes in the tray can still hold interest. They need, in addition, paper for writing on, keeping diaries, the use of a tape recorder and where possible, even an old typewriter will be useful. The more expensive items can often be found at school or in a club if they are not available at home.

The many educational toys that a child of 5 enjoys in order to explore shape, size, colour and texture have not been included in this list; nor have the host of construction sets, games and puzzles enjoyed by older children. These educational and entertainment types of toy or game are excellent for building up a sense of achievement, but unlike the other toys listed above, they do not especially contribute to the release of tension. Some computer games bring release but others may increase frustration; care has to be taken to help the child make the right choice when there is heightened tension. Toys for tension release need not necessarily be expensive. Substitutes can often be found from waste material. They include things that father and mother can make, save or share, or the child can make for himself.

These tension releasing activities and the parents' role in them need to be explained in more detail. Many children, even up to 10 years old, find it easier to express their stressful feelings in play rather than in words. They need to act out these feelings as well as test their dangerous emotions in as harmless a way as possible. The younger the child the easier it is to let him express his hurt through substitutes such as playthings.

When parents are at hand they can do no harm by watching with interest BUT THEY SHOULD NEVER SUGGEST WHAT A CHILD SHOULD DO OR HOW HE SHOULD DO IT. Their role is to supply the material for the game and then accept what is done without criticism or suggestions of their own. If left to his own devices a child will often act out his feelings in a way he finds helpful and by a method that leaves him feeling secure. When tension is very high, then reassurance from his parents that it is safe and in order for him to show how he feels by the way he plays, is all that is needed.

Examples follow of different types of play. They show how they can help parents understand their deeper and not so obvious value.

Example 1 – The use of dolls

A great deal can be learned by listening to children playing with and talking to their dolls. It is usually easy to identify who the doll is supposed to be and what problem the child is working out through his play. Even when the child is playing alone, dolls provide an excellent means of tension release.

Example 2 – The use of sand, water, mud and clay

These materials are often associated with food and toilet-training and they can serve many purposes. Through them, parents can find valuable clues to a child's attitude to his body: worries that are seldom verbalised but which can show up in his play.

Jill, aged 5, had a mother who was an excellent housewife and who was particularly keen on order and cleanliness. She was becoming increasingly concerned over Jill's lateness in being toilet-trained. Rewards for success, ignoring mistakes and avoiding recrimination had all been tried in vain. On advice, Jill's mother began encouraging play with sand and water. Jill rejected the sand and chose mud instead. This she moulded into a squashy mess, adding more and more water. With a naughty grin she said, "Ha ha, just look what I've done. It's mine but I'll give some to you, here, take it".

"I'll hold out my hand. You'd like to see me playing mud-pies too?"

"Now you're all dirty. I'll tell you a secret. It's really a very nice pudding. You eat some." The game of pretence continued with mother being ordered about: "You can't have any more, and mind, don't slop it around. Listen when I tell you things".

97

Jill's mother merely reflected what her daughter said and accepted the game at its face value. Many days of not only playing with mud but mincing up potato peelings and moulding sticky dough, all with mother's approval, resulted in the end in satisfactory toilet control within six weeks. In this instance, Jill worked through her mixed feelings and fears using mud to symbolise her food and excreta and finding reassurance from her mother's presence.

This is no panacea for all cases of slow toilet-training but when a child shows reluctance to handle sand, water, dough, Plasticine or clay, it is a danger signal. Every child needs to be encouraged to do this and know that messy play can be approved by mother. Indeed, a mother might proudly announce that her child is so nice and clean that she will never play with anything messy. The child, inside herself, may well feel 'in a mess' and be striving to be over clean to hide her anxieties even from herself.

Then there was the case of Lorna who tidied everything away, even crumbs, dust, toys and her clothes. She insisted on washing each time she thought she was dirty. This happened some twenty to thirty times a day. Her mother at first thought it was a case of enjoying turning on the taps, but after three tablets of soap had been used in a week it became more than a joke. At the same time Lorna often woke at night screaming and took a long time before she would settle down again. A friend, who had used Tension Release methods with her own child gave her some advice, "You know, you are a pretty fastidious sort of person. Without meaning to you have probably put the idea in Lorna's head that you disapprove when she is dirty. Interest her in mixing dough, it's easier to organise than mud; besides it will be a case of cooking like Mummy".

This advice was taken but it was only after much reassurance and encouragement that Lorna was persuaded that it was fun to knead and touch dough. Once her mother showed her approval, Lorna became delighted with this play activity and entered into it wholeheartedly. In quite a short time Lorna's fears lessened, the nightmares stopped and the obsession with washing disappeared within a few months.

A mother's role is sometimes that of a silent onlooker, merely nodding and smiling to show approval and give reassurance. Dick, aged 4, had no particular problems but there were still anxieties that he never expressed, yet these found an outlet in his play. He made a long roll of Plasticine and while he was playing with it, he chanted:

"Tiddle-de-dee, here's my wee,
As long as a sausage as big as Daddy's."

He was, in fact, reassuring himself that all was well and that he would grow up like Daddy. He had been constantly reproved for clutching his genitals in moments of embarrassment, and this obviously had made him feel guilty and fearful of punishment. While he sang his little ditty he glanced at mother and her approving smile gave him all the reassurance he needed.

Example 3 – Using the model scene

This is a popular and most useful piece of apparatus. It can be used to reduce stress as well as to give countless clues to a child's natural anxieties.

It consists of a set of small models representing the world as a child knows it. Miniature houses, trees, wild and domestic animals, fences, cars, buses, lorries, men, women, soldiers and policemen, boys and girls, cowboys and indians, space people, Spiderman and Superman, circus people and monsters, all need to be collected and used with a small sand tray.

The models are expensive to buy but they can be made by cutting out pictures which can then be stuck in the sand with toothpicks. Children enjoy making these models themselves and are usually unconcerned over their quality as long as they are recognisable.

A child, with the slightest encouragement and perhaps a simple example usually enjoys setting up a scene of his own and spontaneously offers to tell a story about what is happening. "Let's make a picture with all these models and tell a story about what is happening", is the sort of encouragement that is needed.

Mother or father can watch with interest and sometimes reflect the feelings of the various animals and people depicted. Their interest should be devoid of any criticism of what is happening. Educational comment or suggestions as to what comes next should be avoided. This picture scene can be used as a 'special time' game as care is needed to keep the models in good condition. If the apparatus is considered a treat, then children look forward to using it and take great pride in collecting new models. An example of its use follows:

Geoffrey, an overactive, aggressive boy of 5 years old set up a house in the sand, then he carefully fenced it in, put trees all round and introduced what he called 'a wild elephant' which proceeded to break everything to pieces (in pretence). Eagerly the child described what was happening: "The wild elephant is going to jump on the house and squash it to bits and all the people are going to be squashed flat".

His father, who was looking on, commented: "It looks as if the elephant is very angry". He may wonder who the elephant is meant to be but there is no need to ask this question. His comment reflecting what the child's play showed was quite sufficient. The mere acceptance by the parent that these aggressive, rampaging feelings can, and do, exist was enough. The fact that the elephant may represent the child, a parent, a relative or teacher is irrelevant at this stage. What has to be avoided is the game being turned into a natural history lesson on elephants and what they will or will not do in reality. Some parents might feel that such a lesson on animal behaviour would be reassuring but in fact it might have the opposite effect. What the child wants to hear is that his story provokes interest and is accepted. All that is needed might be this: "Oh, what an interesting elephant! I like your story. Do you want to tell me more about what is going to happen?".

The educational line is often hard to resist because it is an adult's natural response to a child's mistaken ideas. This corrective education has its place, but not when a child is trying to release tension. So when a child says "Look at my giant giraffe" and points to an elephant, the correct response would be "Tell me about YOUR giant giraffe", rather than a discourse on the difference between an elephant and a giraffe.

If parents find comment difficult, then it is better to keep quiet, to nod and smile, or simply say "That's fine" or "What's going to happen now?". Any comments that are loaded with what the parent feels himself are completely out of place. For instance, if the father's comment on the elephant was, "Oh, how dreadful! What a horrible animal!" it might well spoil the whole game. The words 'dreadful' and 'horrible' might be the very opposite of what the child had in mind. They could be the very responses the child feared hearing from his parents. Such comments are likely to confuse or arouse anxiety and may well completely inhibit further play.

Example 4 – The use of painting, colour or form
Painting is another form of therapeutic play suitable for children of all ages. Bright colours applied with fingers or big brushes on newspaper or rough paper sheets will serve the purpose. Even a whitewashed wall can be used so long as the limit of "This wall only" is clear!

This activity is not learning to paint but a way to allow a child to express his feelings in colour. Painting at school may, or may not, be a suitable substitute, all depending on how directive the teaching methods are.

At home, parents need do no more than provide the materials, old clothes and a place where mess will not matter. Parental interest and encouragement and a willingness to display the pictures will keep most children happy and eager to continue to experiment. No suggestions or advice, no comments on how the pictures should look, are needed. The result is likely to look like nothing except a messy piece of abstract art. Sometimes, however, the meaning is obvious. Sometimes a child will draw a brother, sister, father or mother, a friend or pet and then splash on red paint, perhaps tear the painting up or even stamp on it. Release of stress in instances like this is clear but more often than not the meaning or benefit is less obvious. But even if this cannot be understood the release of tension that will have taken place is well worthwhile.

Painting is a medium that a child must accept for himself. The materials can be made available but if he asks for his parents to draw they need to avoid doing so and try to get the child to be the active participant. The only reassurance needed is that the picture can be as pretty or ugly as he likes. It does not need to be the kind he draws at school and he needs to be told that whatever he draws will be of interest. Praising the artistic merit may be out of place. A child can be invited to tell what the picture is about and encouraged to do so but never pushed if he seems unwilling.

Example 5 – Tension release through music and movement

Like painting, this medium of tension release can be used only by children who can find expression through it without feeling self-conscious. It is in order when introducing this type of play to demonstrate any kind of movement, mime or dance and then invite the child to join in until he has enough confidence to make up his own steps. It is important to stress to the child that there is no right or wrong way and that any feelings like being happy, sad, angry, worried, quiet or noisy, rough or timid can be shown through dancing, singing or playing musical instruments. The idea that a dance can be like a story, a mime, may be new to some children and they may, as a result, need a few suggestions and demonstrations when they start.

Rhythm, loud and soft noises, made perhaps on a simple drum, cymbals or a mouth-organ, whistle or comb can bring a sense of relaxation to a child as well as releasing some tension. Making music, miming or dancing usually comes easier in the company of other children but just being able to shout, drum or make a noise is often in itself sufficient to help a child get rid of stress. For obvious reasons where and when this release takes place need to be fixed by mutual agreement!

The relaxation found in rhythmic dancing is well known to be an excellent form of release for teenagers. Even very small children in Africa find dance comes naturally. They show gaiety, excitement, anger and pleasure through movement without any prompting or tuition. There is no reason why this activity, so full of free expression, should not be encouraged at home from the earliest age. Just as with painting, this free dance activity at home should not be confused with formal lessons in music, dancing, judo or yoga. All of these may benefit the child and parent but cannot replace spontaneous enjoyment that is part of completely unorganised 'play' at home.

Example 6 – Finding tension release through writing

Once a child shows interest in making up stories, poems, or keeping a diary, he has to hand a simple method of lessening stress. With teenagers, parents have to be very careful not to pry into this sort of activity, but only listen or look when invited and then take the same understanding responsive approach. Once moralising or criticising creep in, the opportunity to help is lost and communication breaks down. People's thoughts and fantasies, wishes and desires are their own business and unlike misbehaviour, parents should be totally permissive over accepting and listening to them even if they are not to their taste.

Billy, aged 14, was always saying "Why can't I have such and such?". His parents were sick and tired of his endlessly nagging them to provide what they could ill afford. Billy was good at English and his teacher, who detected his rebelliousness, suggested writing in his spare time as an outlet. He wrote this story:

"Two worse parents no boy ever had! They were cruel, ugly, mean and greedy but one day he woke up to find a letter, secretly delivered by a stranger. It told him the great news that he had, originally, been adopted. Whoopee! — these terrible people were not really his parents. He left at once on a great adventure to find his new and hopefully, rich home . . . "

Billy, in answer to his father's queries about his interest in writing a book, said that he was only starting on rough plans, "You can't just write a book. I'm starting on short stories".

FATHER: "That's an interesting start."
BILLY: "You mean you like it?"
FATHER: "Of course, but that boy must have felt his Mother and Father were horrible."
BILLY: "They certainly were. Mean as hell, too."
FATHER: "It's terrible to think that people can be treated so badly. Many people do feel that they are, you know."
BILLY: "It's obvious, isn't it? There is so much everyone wants and other people always seem to have more than the not-so-well-off boy."
FATHER: "Perhaps, somehow, you feel we should give you more?". This opened the floodgates:
BILLY: "Well, you could afford it. You bought a car last year, an expensive one, too. My bike isn't even a modern one."

Billy's resentment is now out in the open; communication is established and a discussion on pocket money, earning extra in the holidays, the family budget in general, can take place with some hope of mutually agreed decisions being reached. It is only after tension has eased that a rational conversation, airing the child's, as well as the parents' side of the problem, can take place. This conflict over material things is one of the most pressing questions facing parents and it cannot be solved by reason on the one hand and nagging resentment on the other. Billy, once in a more receptive frame of mind, was alerted to the needs of the whole family and could for the first time, see his own wants and wishes in proportion.

Writing stories may not always be popular but keeping a diary is something many young people enjoy. The privacy of a diary must always be respected. However, a child can be invited to talk about the sort of things he finds worth recording without asking to see the diary itself. Even if parents never see it, all is not wasted. Their respect for their child's privacy will be appreciated and in writing the diary the child may well shed a lot of stress. Quite a few children offer to read out extracts when not pressed to do so and these can, quite deliberately, be very revealing indeed.

Poetry is the medium through which a limited number of children best express their feelings. For example, Henry, aged 9, refused to let his mother out of his sight once he got back from school. The poem he wrote gave a clue to some of the feelings that were causing this lack of independence:

> "I'm still very small
> But one day I will be very old
> Old as my Mum
> Who sometimes cries and cries
> But only with dry eyes."

Henry's grandmother had died a month previously and his mother had tried to protect him from her own sense of loss. She avoided any queries about death although it was obvious that the child was puzzled and frightened by seeing his mother cry. Once his parents realised their mistake, the whole subject of dying was no longer taboo and it gave Henry the chance to express his real fears. These turned out to centre on the fact that his mother might die too as she was undoubtedly getting old like his grandmother.

Example 7 – Tape-recording as a means of reducing stress

Tape-recorders are now commonplace and can be of great use in reducing stress, especially for teenagers. Recorders provide a welcome way to be able to talk about the most disapproved and otherwise impossible things. The ability to play it back and then rub it out makes the process all the more satisfying. It is a form of self-reflection and a young person needs little encouragement to experiment with this medium.

Children with particular problems always want a listening ear but they only dare speak their mind to an impersonal ear like a recorder. Often they secretly wish that their parents could hear. A tape, left to be found 'accidentally on purpose' was made by Denis, a 14 year old whose self-esteem was at a very low ebb:

"It's hard to talk at nothing but anyway I do it all the time in my head. Mum and Dad switch me off often enough; at least this monster won't answer back or slap me down. Who cares what it thinks? Only me, a fat pimply something or other, well I might as well say it, a slug with no shape. Dumpling they call me. Ma says it's a pet name. Rotten, cruel and downright wicked to call anyone a name like that. Bad as that boy they call Cocky and everyone sneers. At least for me it is only Dumps at home. Is it home? Doesn't feel like it. This stupid, stuck-up house, so neat and tidy, it's not the place for me, that's for sure. Meant for stuck-up blokes, not louts like me. And where, Mr Dumps, is the right place? Nowhere. There's nothing to do, nothing to think about, they just order me around like a kid. They spout a lot of lies, but I'm not lying. Why should I? I can rub this out, anyway. I hate them all, they hate me, small doubt about that. Maybe I can find a desert island? Oh gosh, that's kid's stuff. I don't seem to be able to talk to anyone except this machine. Bloody machine! Not sure what I think anymore, well that's it for now my boy, Denis the menace, over and out . . . ".

This tape gave a lot of insight into Denis' damaged self-image. His parents played the tape in genuine error, thinking it was one of their own that had been borrowed. The tape came as a big shock and they lost no time facing Denis with what had happened. Surprisingly, his anger was short-lived and the whole affair led to communication opening up on nicknames, their expectations of him and his of himself. The spring of tension slowly began to unwind and school work, as well as home relationships, improved.

Example 8 – *Making use of acting and role-taking*

Children of all ages enjoy dressing up and playing parts. They love taking off their parents and other grown-ups, exaggerating their faults and highlighting irritating habits. A lot of good can come of this if parents take part or are invited to these small plays. This is, naturally, half the fun for the young. It is fatal for hurt feelings to show and criticisms or self-defence to creep in. An embarrassing silence or unpleasant argument is the likely result if they do. On the other hand, if all is taken in good part, the way is open for friendly discussion.

More often, the children, if left to their own devices, act out small plays using general situations, rather than real ones that actually exist in the family. However, with young children, acting out a specific problem can be used in a crisis. For example: Pam, aged 3, stubbornly refuses to eat breakfast. In fact, she flings it away as mother hurries off to catch a bus for work. "You mustn't go. You naughty Mummy!" Her father listens responsively and says, "You feel angry with Mummy because she has to go out to work".

"I won't finish my food."

"We'll finish eating together, but let's have a pretend game. You can be Mummy" and he throws over her mother's apron. Pam gets off her chair, head in air, and goes out slamming the door. She opens it a crack and peeps in. "Ha, ha, I went out and left you all alone".

"You look just like Mummy. She will peep in at the door too, after work and we'll all be together again." Pam, relaxed and relieved, sits down and eats her toast. The fear at the back of her mind that mother may be abandoning her soon fades when she acts out the part of her mother's return, and is reassured by her father's understanding.

From 7 to 12 years old, acting with the family is usually a lighthearted affair, usually initiated by the children, with lots of fun and laughter thrown in. It is not merely a matter of 'taking the mickey' out of the grown-ups, but is a process of working out problems of relationships and testing out reactions.

In one family where parental quarrels were common, youngsters demanded that their parents play the part of their children and so were made to face whose side to take when a 'parental row' was in progress.

Children's anxieties are lessened when they see that their parents can laugh at themselves and can meet the same sort of problems that face the young. In role-taking games, many sensitive areas of family, school and social life can be brought into the open and through acting them out, solutions found and reassurance given. Some families make a habit of exploring problems in this way. Children find role-play a particularly useful way of exploring those areas of behaviour that most perplex them in real life. Strangers, amorous boys, seductive girls, unreasonable teachers or friends who are disloyal, all provide common role-taking subjects which the young find most helpful. This kind of acting-game solution is sometimes easier than a straight discussion because it is less personal and several alternative ways of solving the problem can be tried out.

You-And-Me-Alone-Time

Play at home gives parents a big chance to gain insight into how their children feel and it can help in solving some of their inevitable growing up problems. Yet many parents are disbelieving, as was this mother who declared, "Oh, but my child never says anything like that or plays in that sort of way".

In these cases one wonders how much watching and listening to children at play goes on; probably not much. One also wonders what interesting talk and play goes on, while parents are at work; probably a great deal. Time and opportunity for keeping in touch with children at play is something parents have to consider and plan for in a busy life. Even on a crowded day a 'you-and-me-alone-time' with each young child is a must. Mealtimes together are no substitute for this.

During this special 'together-time' the child can choose what he wants to do. These precious moments belong to him. It is the parent's chance to feed in all the emotional foods the child needs, by word and gesture. It is a time when the child is the very centre of attention. There is no other time to compare with it. School may give varying opportunities for play, but nothing can take the place of the close interaction of parent and child during you-and-me-alone-time.

How is this special time started? With very young children there is no difficulty whatsoever; they take to it like a fish to water. Parents can say,

"Mummy and Daddy are very busy people. I am sure you would like them to stop being so busy and to put aside a time when we could be alone together and do whatever you want. It will be your time and you can choose what to do".

How long should it be and when? These are personal questions that concern time available and inclination which can only be answered by individual parents. Everyone's life is organised to a different pattern, but just as every parent finds time for other essentials, surely they can make time for this invaluable 'you-and-me-alone' period. It is a time that a child should be able to count on absolutely. It is worth going to great lengths to make it an undisturbed ten or fifteen minutes, on however many days parents feel they can manage. But it must be certain and it must be regular. It means no telephone, no visitors, no buts and can'ts, no "I'll be back in a moment" or "Just wait a second".

This time alone should be in addition to 'bed-time' which is often the only together time with father and generally includes a story or chatter with two or more children together. The two types of time together serve two different purposes. 'Bed-time' is a quiet preparation for sleep and reassurance against the fear of separation, whereas 'you-and-me-alone' time should be stimulating, active or comforting, as the child dictates. It should take place any time during the day except bedtime.

How can this time be used? The child chooses exactly what he wishes to do. If he is at a loss and asks for a suggestion the safest answer is, "You say", even if a wide variety of choices is then offered. Activities can be indirectly steered into play where the child takes the active role or gains comfort from cuddling, bossing or ordering his parent about. Whatever happens he needs to feel he can say what he likes and be free to express feelings that might normally bring the response: "Mummy will listen some other time, darling".

Reassurance about games not having to be played with any particular rules, dolls not having to be well-behaved or pictures necessarily pretty, help the child feel safe over airing any feelings of hurt, fear or hostility. It is certainly one of the best ways to help a child suffering from jealousy after a new arrival in the family. Quite apart from providing tension release it gives parents a chance to give extra love and reassurance that the elder child is valued for himself. Also, when difficult behaviour alerts that all is not well, this time together gives a special opportunity to watch for clues as to what the cause may be.

Everyone at some stage reaches the point of not being able to see the wood for the trees; they know something is wrong but their child is unable to tell them what it is, and they feel helpless to understand or deal with the cause.

106

Older children still want short times of individual attention when they can talk and share their interests. Watching television has robbed many a family of this time together, but even if telly is a must at least it can be watched together and programmes discussed, the initiative being left to the children.

A random example of 'you-and-me-together-time' will help to show the use that can be made of it, by both parent and child. Leslie came back from nursery school in a grumpy mood and he and his elder sister were bickering at each other the whole time; his mother thought that the children would benefit by being separated:

"Time for our all-alone ten minutes, Leslie."

"Great. But tell Diana she can't join in."

"Time alone means you and me alone. She will have her turn later. You seem to be having a go at each other today."

"She is a bossy cat and interferes. I can do some things better than she can."

"Come on then, what do you want to do today?"

"Mmmm . . . let me think. Let's have a record."

"What would you like?"

"The Sound of Music! Can you help me put it on?"

They sat on the sofa and this was an excuse to cuddle up and feel close and loved. He held his mother's hand, kissed her and enjoyed being kissed back. This went on for a short time while he hummed to the music very happily. Then he asked to play Snap. But each time mother won some cards he became cross. "You always win. It's not fair."

"You feel you should win?", his mother said, using Responsive Listening.

"Diana always wins. I didn't even win at school today."

"Did that feel bad?"

"It's best to win, isn't it? Let's play jumping over the pouffe."

"You're very good at that, aren't you?". He demonstrates his prowess but makes no move to suggest mother competing.

"My teacher says I can be good at anything if I try, but it's no good saying that and then not letting me win."

"You feel the teacher isn't fair?"

"No. She only chooses Lynn because she is a girl."

"The teacher likes girls best?"

"Girls always get the best of it. You musn't hit a girl. You musn't mess up their hair or dirty their posh clothes. Cissies, that's what they are."

"You feel all girls are cissies?"

"Of course all girls are. You are a cissy too, sometimes. Come on, let's play with the cars. I'll have the Land Rover and you have the Mini." They roll them and see which goes the furthest.

This short 'time-alone-together' had allowed Leslie to express his frustration over competing with an older sister and perhaps gave his mother a hint that they were expecting too much of him. He was setting his own sights too high and still had to learn a reasonable compromise. His mother was given the chance to cuddle and caress him which she knew he wanted and enjoyed but ordinarily brushed aside as 'cissy'. Opportunities for showing demonstrative affection in a natural sort of way were hard to find, but in the 'you-and-me-alone' time he felt able to be his own age and to accept cuddles. Reassurance of his own worth had also given him enough confidence to express some of his school problems where his self-esteem had taken a knock.

When discussing the value of time alone, Leslie's mother said she found it one of the most useful ways to learn Responsive Listening. She had been tempted to tell her son that he couldn't possibly expect to win all the time, that it was nonsense to feel that a teacher would favour a girl and still more nonsense to call all girls cissies. She saw, quite clearly, that had she allowed herself to say all this, true as it was, Leslie's reaction would have been antagonistic and the happy time alone would have ended in a battle. As it was, he had begun to work things out for himself through his own play.

To sum up: Play activity, of any of the types described, helps to reduce stress. This is true whether a child has a particularly pressing problem or only a general background of those lesser tensions which always arise in the normal course of life. The play, in itself, releases tension but there is an added bonus if parents are present. If they behave and respond without criticism then the confidence of the child is increased and this will encourage him to express his feelings more openly.

Parents can find additional benefits from observing and sometimes participating in the play. In their role as responsive listeners they can encourage further communication. This, in turn, enables them to become detectives, recognising and interpreting the messages and clues which point towards problem areas. Once these areas are clearly identified then positive action can be taken to deal with them, with the comforting reassurance that they are no longer floundering in the dark.

CHAPTER 12 : Parents Need To Have Their Say
Children Need To Listen

Parents Need Consideration Too

Up to this point, the emphasis has been placed on the part parents have to play to keep tension down and to build warm relationships with their children. The skills they have to learn, the emotional food they have to provide, the understanding they have to show, all have been covered and explained.

So far it seems a very one-sided effort with the adults doing it all. As a result, there may be a justifiable outcry from parents, "What about us? We also get into a state, feel tired, irritated, frustrated, impatient and even angry! There are dozens of practical needs of our own that clash with our childrens' wishes every day. We have our own set of adult problems that get us hot under the collar too, plus the load and the responsibility of providing for our family. Is this whole process of family life ever a two-way system? What about teaching the kids some skills? Shouldn't they know how to cool us down and make us feel good about ourselves? Surely too, children can be expected to show a bit of understanding!".

These views are absolutely reasonable. However, it is unfortunate but true, that although children do not enjoy irritable and angry parents, left to themselves they will do little about it. They are much more concerned with satisfying their own needs and momentary whims.

Can they be taught to be more thoughtful and show more empathy for their parents? Happily there is some motivation for children to respond to some of their parents' needs. There is their own wish for self-esteem, their liking of feeling kind and helpful, their wish to be loved and approved of and their knowledge, born of experience, that warm relationships bring happiness. All these factors work in the right direction for parents.

A young child will volunteer with sincerity, "Mum, I want to please you. I want to see you happy; it gives me a comforting sort of feeling". There are many tender moments, too, in every family.

"You look dead beat, Mum. Let me do the ironing."

"I can see you need help, Dad. I'll drop what I'm doing and give you a hand."

"Sssh — do be quiet. Mum's got a headache."

These tender, loving and thoughtful reactions that come naturally are a bonus that can be built on. This calls for yet further efforts from parents but the rewards make it worthwhile. There is no doubt that children can be taught and encouraged to listen and to respond to their parents' pleas, to show empathy and understanding of their parents' problems and to carry their fair share in building warm relationships. Let us see how this can be done.

109

Social initiatives or volunteered help from children are only in evidence when a feeling of relaxation predominates and no conflict of other interests is strong enough to intervene. This is why all the tension-releasing skills have been dealt with first. Once these skills have been put into practice then parents have a much better chance of getting their children to listen, to be less selfish and more ready to comply with adults' wishes.

Right from his earliest years, when a child is beginning to talk, he can be helped to be aware that there are two sides to most of the conflicting needs that always exist in any family. For example, comments like these can sow the right seeds: "You like your toys spread all over the lounge. Mummy feels upset if things aren't tidy when Dad comes home or friends call".

"You like to run around with no pants on because it feels nice and cool. Mummy likes you to dress like everyone else when you go to the playground because people expect me to dress you properly."

"You like the television on all the time. I like it on only when there is something we particularly like to watch."

Parents need to show their wishes quite clearly, but express them, not as a direct order, but as a PLEA seeking the child's cooperation. For example, "Chrissie, when I'm talking to Mrs. Smith I feel rude if I have to keep interrupting her to talk to you".

"When you keep getting out of bed and disturbing me, I can't get Daddy's dinner ready and he will be hungry when he comes in."

Clear but indirect pleas of this kind are often met by the child simply because he wants to please the person he loves. He is motivated to please because he wants someone on whom he can count and trust to give him support and affection. From these small beginnings a child's total self-centredness gives way to a realisation of other people's reactions and needs. This gradually develops until it forms the basis of concern for others including wider social implications and obligations. With proper guidance he will end up with a fully developed awareness of the needs of mankind as a whole.

A child begins to develop a conscience during his first year and the process continues until he reaches the stage where he feels uncomfortable when he fails to conform to his own code of values. His code develops very naturally. He finds that his actions are appreciated or not noticed, are called right or wrong, kind or unkind. Sharing meets with approval, pinching or hitting meets with disapproval and so on. He wants to be liked and he feels pleasure if he does something that brings approval or reward. In the same way he is less inclined to repeat anything that he knows will bring pain or disapproval. As the child grows older, consideration and the ability to see another person's point of view become desirable qualities. They make for friendliness and warm relationships, whereas being selfish has the opposite effect.

Once parents appreciate how this code of conduct and conscience builds up, they have a marvellous opportunity to guide the social development of their children in satisfactory directions. Any action by their children showing consideration for others needs to be noticed and encouraged by recognition and pleasure. In this way it will become part of a natural behaviour pattern. If a start is made in the early years and conscientiously followed through the growing-up period, then parents will soon find that raising a family need not be a one-sided affair with all the load falling on them, but rather a cooperative effort by all.

As well as being guided by parents and learning from his own experience, a child who sees people he loves performing acts of kindness, being fair, unselfish, generous and considerate, will be encouraged to imitate them. Gradually these ways of behaviour become part of the child's own code of values. He will, of course, respond in the same way, copying unsatisfactory examples.

In a home where positive values are clear and adhered to by the parents, where there is warmth, no constant ordering, threatening or insisting, the ground is easily prepared for a child to listen and show concern for others. By the time the naturally assertive years of the 2's and 3's and the growing independence of the 4's, 5's and 6's are reached, there can be a wealth of ways by which a child finds it is a pleasure to be cooperative.

As time passes and the chance for coercion by parents diminishes, the advantage of having set the right pattern in the earlier years becomes evident. By the late teens a certain amount of self-discipline and social responsibility are usually in evidence.

How To Encourage Children To Listen

There are two main factors which influence whether or not children will listen to a plea by their parents. The first is that the general atmosphere has to be one that will not ask for annoyance and arguments. The second is the form the plea itself takes. The preceding chapters have dealt with setting a climate of consideration, so the form of the plea will now be described.

By its very nature, a plea should not be in the form of a demand or even a direct request. It needs to be a parent's indirect call for considerate action in response to how the parent is FEELING. There should be no room for doubt about how they feel. This needs to be stated clearly and accurately but not exaggerated. The plea should help the child put himself in the parent's shoes. It should call for his sympathy and so make it easier for him to comply. For clarity, some examples follow: "When you climb on that high wall, it really worries me because you may fall and hurt yourself badly." This is quite different from the command which attracts defiance: "You must not climb on that high wall. You may fall and hurt yourself".

Another plea could be directed at the reckless way a child rides his bike. "When I see you going at that speed straight onto the main road, I nearly go crazy with worry, and I can't settle to anything till you are back." This is more likely to succeed than, "I forbid you to ride your bike so fast".

These are only two examples of the almost countless number of pleas that can be made to arrest worrying behaviour and gain cooperation. In a family where orders have been the norm then even a well-expressed plea will not produce miracles. Antagonism and refusal to comply can be expected. The negative aspect of the home has to change before there is much chance of an indirect plea being successful.

When parents finally open up their minds to the need for change, they may well ask, "Can we, at this late stage, ever undo all the mistakes we have made? Shall we be able in a reasonable amount of time, to get our children to listen and voluntarily meet our demands?". The answer is that the task may not be as gigantic as it appears, but naturally the turnabout will not happen overnight. Warming relationships and cooling tempers, as described,   are something positive to work on as soon as possible.

Children may be surprised and suspicious of any sudden change in approach to relationships. Such proposed changes need to be fully discussed, and with teenagers, their opinions sought on how best to proceed. Some light-hearted chatter about how best to avoid falling back into the old way, never does harm.

The skill needed to make successful pleas is much less than that for Responsive Listening. This is because it has to do with "I" as the parent and how "I" feel, how it affects "ME" and why. There is no need to guess, as one knows exactly how one feels and what one wants.

One danger is that feelings may be exaggerated. A parent may say he feels 'furious', when he is mildly annoyed. On the other hand feelings may be played down. A parent may claim that he is a 'bit scared' when he is, in fact, extremely worried. Parents soon learn that a child listens and responds more readily when what is said about feelings is as near the truth as possible.

The Form A Plea Should Take

Forming a plea is yet another skill to learn. As a first step it will be easiest, when practising, to start the sentence with the words "WHEN I . . .". This is not essential once the skill is mastered but it certainly helps a novice to start the plea correctly. It is the emphasis on the "I" that matters, leading to what "I" want.

This start of "WHEN I . . . " is then followed by a description of the behaviour the plea hopes to change; this, in turn, is followed by what the parent feels if the disturbing behaviour continues. The plea is rounded off by a statement giving the reason why the parent feels as he does.

Some examples may help to make the different parts of a plea stand out more clearly:

"When I am on the phone . . . and you keep interrupting me . . . I get annoyed . . . because I can't hear what the person on the phone is saying."

"When I am in a hurry to go out . . . and you mess about . . . I get irritated . . . because I will miss my bus."

"When I am busy . . . and you keep asking questions . . . I get irritated . . . because I won't get through all my jobs."

This four-part sequence is suggested when learning, as it avoids the danger of slipping in the words "You MUST . . . " in the centre of the plea. For example: "When I am on the phone, YOU MUST keep quiet or I will not be able to hear". The start of this plea is fine and if there is a climate of good cooperation then the child may comply. The drawback is that the solution is given in the form of a command and this may annoy some children and cause them to be contrary. The older a child the less he likes to be told "YOU MUST". In fact, everyone prefers to feel that they are free to choose rather than being ordered to do something.

Another reason for resistance arises when the reason the parent gives for making his plea is not valid, "When I see your hair so matted and untidy I feel ashamed because it looks so awful". A teenager is unlikely to respond to such an indirect plea to tidy his hair and may well reply: "Why feel ashamed? It's my hair. I like it and so do my friends. Surely how I do my hair is my business? I don't ask Dad to go around in old jeans when he joins me and my friends, even though we feel he looks silly and stuffy all dressed up as he is". So if there is any doubt about the feelings or reasons for a plea being accepted it is better left unsaid.

When Children Fail To Respond

Even when expressed correctly, pleas from parents can be met with a flat refusal to comply: "I don't care what you feel. I want to do it". Or, "I don't want to. So why should I?".

When this happens the best thing to do is to repeat the plea more assertively and maybe repeat it several times in a slightly different form. The use of first names may help to call special attention, or a look or a tone which reinforces the plea is sometimes helpful:

"Look, Ann, I really mean it . . . "

"Do you understand? It is really important to me . . . "

"I'm telling you once again . . . "

If this fails then stress the feelings that are aroused and check if A THREAT, A COMMAND or A MUST are included in the unsuccessful plea. If all of these suggestions have been tried and the plea still fails, then the last and only line of action left, is to fall back on tension release. Any negative response to a plea needs to be met by Responsive Listening.

It is very difficult to revert to Responsive Listening in the face of repeated pleas being turned down. Feelings of exasperation, worry and fear tend to be running high by that stage. It is, however, the only way and parents need to accept this as fact. Nothing will convince them but their own experience and so, when all else has failed, they should give this method a chance.

Perseverance is an essential ingredient. Reflecting back what the child is feeling may have to be repeated for some minutes before success is achieved. In the face of continued understanding, resistance often evaporates quite suddenly, when all hope of a breakthrough has gone. It is as if the child says to himself: "There is Dad getting all steamed up, but at least he sees my point of view even if he is upset. I'd better do what he wants". A child's surprise and satisfaction at a parent's persistent show of understanding can work magic!

Making a correct indirect plea, avoiding all the pitfalls and even resorting to Responsive Listening when faced with stubborn resistance, may still not be enough. Research has shown that failure to respond to a reasonable plea is a clear indication that the level of permanent tension has reached the point where it cannot be broken down by occasional friendliness or appeals for sympathy.

The warning is clear. If indirect pleas fall on deaf ears then a parent needs to examine his total relationship with his child and take positive action to bring more love and understanding into it.

There remains a special kind of behaviour that is common enough to warrant attention. Sheer contrariness and direct disobedience are sometimes so marked that ordinary pleas are met by stubborn refusal and rebellion. Parents ask, when faced with this situation, what can be done immediately to stop trouble escalating?

Many children who have manipulated their parents and got their own way when young, often lose the limelight when they have to compete with brothers and sisters or when mother goes out to work. They feel a powerful need to get back sole attention coupled with a need to seek revenge or pit their strength against an adult by making him angry. Some children will behave like this only if under general stress but others get into the habit of only feeling satisfied if they continually disturb the equilibrium of the home.

There are only two possible replies in these circumstances. One is to take no notice, ignore the child and so refuse to rise to the bait. The other is to hit the nail on the head with a Responsive Listening reflection such as one of these:

"It seems you want to make me angry."

"You are behaving this way to make me cross."

"I know that you can behave sensibly, so I am going to wait until you do just that. Please understand I am not going to lose my temper."

A child bent on disrupting family harmony may have to be restrained or , by mutual agreement, isolated in another room for a while. It is only if he fails to succeed in this disruption or to arouse anger, that his behaviour will change.

The process of accepting only a fair share of the limelight will be a slow one. Each time the errant child catches attention by pleasing instead of disrupting, then he should be rewarded by special attention and appreciation. The sadness is that we parents tend to pay more attention to naughtiness than to reasonable behaviour, which we take for granted. Children soon recognise this and are not slow to capitalise on it.

Should Parents Say How Angry They Feel?

The way has been described by which parents may use their own feelings as a means of getting children to respond to their wishes. Does this mean they should describe how they feel even when very angry indeed?

Hot anger is nothing new to a child. They know all too well the feeling of being overwhelmed by the force of their own anger and aggression. They also know that these strong feelings can damage relationships. In addition, when a child feels angry, the object of his anger comes under fire; so when his parents' anger is expressed in strong terms the child may feel that he is a target. As a result, from the child's point of view, the situation might be a frightening one. This may go far beyond what the parents intended. For this reason the words 'very cross' or 'very annoyed' are better than 'furious' or 'extremely angry'. The tone and look give enough indication of how the parent feels without the addition of any label that might have frightening associations for the child. Parents cannot be expected to stifle their feelings and sometimes they let fly on the spur of the moment. As long as they direct their anger at the child's behaviour and not at the child himself, no harm is done.

"When I find you have raided the fridge and eaten the sweet I made for today's party, I feel very cross about what you've done. It (the behaviour) is naughty and thoughtless." This gives a clear picture of how mother feels but it has a different effect on the child than if she had said: "I feel very angry with you. You are very naughty and thoughtless."

Threats about getting angry such as: "I warn you if you do that again, I shall be very angry", often meet with short term success. The child may be so frightened that he will comply. If the motive for compliance is fear, then if the threat is constantly repeated and nothing happens, it becomes a joke and will be ignored.

Similarly, arousing a strong sense of guilt in a child is unwise. For example: "I feel so ashamed of you", "I feel so disappointed in you". This deflates the child's self-esteem and if he does not rebel, it will be his fear, not his wanting to please, that makes him comply.

"I know Mum will be pleased if I do as she wants when she tells me it's important for her." This is the reaction we all long for. We want our children to do something because they know it will please us and make them feel good about themselves. This is so much better than doing what we want them to do because they are scared stiff!

Parents, even more than children, will get extremely bad-tempered if they find no one listens to or takes any notice of their calls for help and co-operation. It is, therefore, worth restating the main points that make children listen and respond to parents' wishes.

1) In the first place, the parent's problem needs to be stated simply and clearly so that there is no doubt that it is understood. The message as to how they want the problem solved also has to be stated.

2) Parents need to mention their expectations and feelings as often as they can as this invites a response from the children and also encourages a wish to please.

3) Patience is needed. A plea may need to be REPEATED several times, with more and more emphasis before it is heeded.

4) In addition, there are several ways to alert children to a plea that will encourage them to respond. These include making sure that the request is heard, even in the normal family hubbub: "Lunch is in five minutes — Listen all of you — Lunch is in five minutes. I'm not going to warn you again".

5) Humour often turns reluctance into a wish to comply. Patrick, aged 13, said: "Mum puts on a comic act and pulls a funny face when I don't listen. It makes us all laugh and there is no way I can refuse to do what she wants".

6) Most important of all, cooperation with parents' wishes comes easily when the atmosphere in the home is relaxed. We can never expect this cooperation and should not ask for it when everyone is feeling rebellious and breathing antagonism. The key to being listened to and helped lies in making sure that all the tension-releasing skills have first been used and then to state the grown-ups' expectations. If these tips are followed then parents can, with confidence, expect the best and not the worst response from their youngsters.

PART 3 FINDING SOLUTIONS

CHAPTER 13: Finding Agreed Solutions Within The Family

The Value Of Discussion

Normal, day-to-day family confrontations can be solved by the use of the tension-releasing skills that have been described. When tension fades, a feeling of togetherness develops and this can be further encouraged by follow-up discussions. Talking together in a relaxed atmosphere has many advantages. We all sense this but somehow our lives seem so busy that we never find the time to let it happen. As parents, we are missing a great opportunity.

Through quiet discussion, ideals and values can be passed on without playing the 'heavy parent' or laying down the law. Relaxed children welcome adults' views especially when their own opinions are heard and respected. Values passed on casually in this way often take root, even if they seem to have fallen on stony ground.

Talking together also creates a natural opportunity for a child to ask about things he needs to know, and which otherwise he may only find out when it is too late. Children often pick up wrong information that needs correcting and they tend only to learn about things that concern them closely. Family discussions can put both these disadvantages to rights while informing as well as warning.

Talk often develops around the right and wrong ways of behaving and the consequences that can follow. Only when the inevitable question is put, "Well Dad, what do you think? Where do you stand, and why?" can a parent feel free to state the rights and wrongs, clearly voicing his viewpoint backed up by reasons.

Those who never express their own positive opinions on the grounds that children should be free to choose without being pushed or influenced, are not being realistic. They are unconsciously influencing their children all the time. In response to direct questions, naturally, they give their ideas on politics, religion and social issues. Anything else would be evasive. Influencing the opinion of a child is quite different from forcing a viewpoint on him.

Finally, discussion is the best way to reach a compromise solution in confrontations where, for instance, a child refuses to respond to a plea. All should be able to have their say and put forward suggested solutions. The participants then feel involved and a party to final decisions. Afterwards they will be more likely to stick by any agreement reached.

Finding mutually-agreed solutions which respect all vested interests in a family is never easy and poses a considerable challenge. If this challenge is taken up there is a real possibility of living together in harmony, and for the children to learn to become self-regulating, responsible individuals.

Is Mutual Agreement Possible With Toddlers?

Until the child can use language adequately, the only solution to many problems is by the use of Limits and Rules as described in Chapter 7. With toddlers the limit of "Biscuits are for eating at tea time only" can be made to stick providing mother perseveres without relenting or getting cross. The position is quite different once the child begins to talk, can climb like Sir Edmund Hillary, and can open cupboards and locks with the ease of Houdini! If on top of all these skills he turns a deaf ear to any plea then the only alternative to buying a lot of biscuits is to try to come to an agreed solution.

Young children's suggested solutions to problems are at first often impractical or ridiculous, but it is surprising at what an early age they begin to come up with reasonable answers to problems. It is equally surprising how well they will stick to any solution to which they have been a party. So the earlier a start is made trying out this method the better. The alternatives of physical force, threats or punishments only increase tension and bring more trouble. They are not short-cuts but just plain short-sighted!

Steps Towards Mutual Agreement

In trying to reach mutual agreement there are five steps that need to be worked through. They read as more tedious and drawn-out than they really are in practice. An example will illustrate these steps. Tim and his mother continually argued over her insistence that he wore wellington boots and not his best shoes when outdoors in the wet. Tim refused to comply, mother was adamant and the argument never-ending. So mother set the ball rolling by trying to find a mutually-agreed compromise solution:

Step 1 — *Listening to the child's point of view*

"Well, Tim, let me hear what you have to say about this problem of not wearing your best shoes in the wet." Mother listens attentively while Tim explains how difficult it is always putting on and taking off his wellingtons.

Step 2 — *The conflict is clearly defined*

Mother defines the conflict: "I can see what a struggle it is for you tugging your boots on and off. Shoes are much easier. For my part I am concerned how to stop expensive shoes getting ruined very quickly in the wet".

Steps 3 and 4 — *Possible solutions and reactions considered*

These two steps are combined, as first solutions are seldom accepted. The discussion could go like this: "Now, Tim, what do you suggest we do?".

"Couldn't you buy me a new pair of wellies with a zip? They'll slip on easily."

"I'm afraid we cannot afford new boots while yours are still fine. Remember you chose them to fit tight."

118

"Well, Mum, we take the same size. Could I borrow your zip ones?"

"I might agree for a special occasion but not for every rainy day. They'd soon be finished and anyway we would both need them at the same time."

"Well, I suppose I could wear my old tennis-shoes in the wet."

"That's a possibility. Can't say I would like the feel or the look of wet plimsolls, but it's your choice."

"At least they will be easy to slip on. I suppose that's the best answer until I am due for new boots."

"O K, Tim. I agree, let's try it."

Step 5 — *Assuring the compromise will be kept*

Solutions agreed may seem fine at the time but agreements can easily be broken. This possibility should be faced at the time they are made.

"We now agree, Tim. What if you forget and go back to your shoes in the wet?"

"Well, we've agreed so I won't fuss if you remind me. I'll keep my old tennis-shoes in a box by the door so they'll be handy." Tim's mother is satisfied and the agreement is on.

Reaching solutions is often condensed in practice. The steps can be combined and step 5 left out with younger children who one expects to break the bargain constantly. Even here, all is not wasted, as the child is at least learning the process. Once a child becomes used to the idea of reaching agreed solutions the time involved becomes less and less. The introduction of this new approach will call for patience if a child has grown up fighting to get his own way.

Finding Solutions As A Group

When the family gets older and joins in helping to run the house then times for doing things are bound to conflict. Interests, needs and values will tend to diverge and as a result there will be many more points of friction and family concerns to settle. The following comments illustrate how easily these areas of friction can arise:

"Mummy is always grumbling about our being late for meals."

"Some kids never have to do any chores. Why should I?"

"I want to learn riding, Bess wants to skate and Bill is mad on his band. Now Dad says he is too broke. What a mess."

"I've asked Pam to spend the day here. Now you have ruined it all by having the twins round as well. Mum will go spare over all the extras for lunch."

"Look, I want to see that film on ITV. You'll have to miss the racing and Dad his golf. I got in first so don't go on creating."

"Why ask us to lend you money for the bus when you just throw yours away on trash? It would help if we knew exactly what our pocket money had to cover."

Any of these complaints might bring home to parents the need for the family to meet as a group to sort out their conflicting interests. In a busy life there is no chance of getting everyone together without fair warning. In addition the whole idea of a family meeting becomes more acceptable if it has a name, meets regularly at a set time and everyone agrees on a date well in advance. The name comes best from the family. 'Council', 'Family Pow-Wow' 'The Crunch', 'The Get-Together' or 'Family Forum' are a few names chosen by different families. These regular meetings can be few in number and take place whether there is any outstanding friction or not. When an immediate crisis arises then an emergency meeting can be called at short notice, possibly limited to those involved. For the time spent to be worthwhile, everyone should be warned well in advance of the agenda. Someone should act as secretary and have paper and pencil to jot down final decisions and the date of the next meeting. Children prefer a definite routine to follow as long as they are sure they will have a chance of airing any grievances about which they have been reluctant to give advance warning. "Any other business" can cater for this.

When teenagers have been brought up to the idea of open discussion, a large range of subjects usually gets raised. There is the crucial question about what the family can afford, the need for transport, special hobbies and activities, pocket money and what it has to cover, sharing the family car, plans over where to spend the family holiday and special treats and individual interests all of these may give rise to conflict. There are plenty of areas where a co-operative effort needs to be agreed upon. Sharing chores, transport, television viewing, punctuality and general tidiness are just a few of the subjects that affect everyone. The list is endless as is the number of views that can be expressed on contemporary problems such as smoking, drugs, drink and dating. Airing these subjects before they reach crisis level can never do harm.

Children will look forward to these family meetings as long as a clear distinction is made between what is a genuine family problem and what is the private concern of the individual. Trying to find compromise solutions about an individual's problems, tastes or life-style — doing homework, working hard at school, preferences for games or reading — is not on! All of these are individual choices and understandable resentment will be aroused if they become the subject of family attack.

Children often ask for facts and figures on various subjects at these family meetings: economic facts, vocational issues, VD, AIDS, the Pill are just a few examples. As long as sensitive subjects are not treated personally (unless advice is asked for) these discussions are invaluable.

Parents have to be especially careful not to preach, snipe or give the impression that anyone who disagrees is disloyal or an outsider. Cliques and alliances need to be spotted before they disrupt the group. If children feel they are being ganged up against, then a walk-out or refusal to attend becomes a real possibility. The family meeting has to be a strengthening experience. Teenagers who are trying to find their own way need support and understanding, rather than the ready-made solutions of another generation.

To help those who have no experience of family meetings, two examples follow. The first shows how the forum was used to handle a simple domestic problem and the second covers a very serious crisis involving the whole family.

Example 1

The mother of a family felt desperate about tidiness in the house. She felt like going on strike over having to clear up everyone's things that were left all over the place. Her pleas to individuals fell on deaf ears. She stated her case at the family meeting in this way: "I know it is easy to chuck things down without thinking, but I really get mad having to clear it all up day after day. When I just leave it the house looks like a pigsty. No one can ever find anything and then you all nag at me! Please, I want some constructive suggestions".

In the course of the discussion that followed, suggestions were made that fell into these three categories:

Let's take it in turns to tidy up;

Let's throw everything in a corner in one pile;

Let's agree to put our own things away.

These suggestions were evaluated and the third was voted the only acceptable one. As good intentions so often go by the board it was vital to decide how to enforce this commonsense solution. Punishments such as fines or extra chores were ruled out as being liable to cause ill-feeling and being too hard to administer. The suggestion that Mum remind everyone was vetoed by Mum! The agreement that everyone took a turn at being the one to remind, a week at a time, was unanimous. A list was then prepared showing the duty roster.

Example 2

This takes the form of a transcript of a tape sent by a husband to a counsellor describing an emergency family meeting which had to deal with the impending break-up of the marriage: "I have tried to get the family together informally to talk things over but without success. Thank heaven for our long-established habit of having family meetings from time to time! Anyway, in desperation I called an emergency gathering and got a full house with no trouble at all once the subject was known! Margaret was, of course, in

Wales and so was not there. She usually manages these family things so I was unsure about how to cope. I'm afraid I'm very much at sea in so many ways and being able to talk to you like this helps tremendously.

To go back to this meeting, at first I had to jolly things along as there is a strict rule that nothing personal is brought up. Karen began by apologising and saying that M. and I separating did impinge on them all and I agreed. I admired her maturity, poor kid, as she assured me they were not going to blame me or ask for us to reconsider. Once I told them that it was important to face all the consequences of the break-up, pendemonium broke loose. I just can't remember the order or who said what, but Des looked grim, and Julia terrified. Roughly they wanted to know a lot of practical things. Where would they live? Would the house be sold? Would I marry again? How would I cope with the 'girly' things? Would they have to cook? Would they have to mend and look after me? And so on and on . . . they didn't even wait for answers! Obviously they were worried stiff that their lives would change for the worse. I hardly got a word in edgeways. I think they sensed my total inability to get to grips with things.

Karen, in a matter of fact sort of way, then said they had plenty of friends whose families had split up and that they were lucky to have me willing to discuss things, as most girls she knew went about walking on hot bricks, not knowing from one moment to another what was going on. I explained the quandary I was in: keen not to blame or justify myself or Margaret, and this was why it was so difficult to bring things out into the open. Des, still very bitter, said Mum and I had been like cat and dog and was I mad enough to think they hadn't noticed? Can you believe it, little Julia piled in with: "That's an attack! It's not fair, it's not allowed!"

After that I pulled myself together and told Karen to write down the main problems. They then formulated them and dammit, the legal position in this interim two years' separation, the financial side, what choice they had over material things, what was the agreed story for them to tell their friends, and then later, would they see Mum as much as they wanted, and how would it all work in a practical way? In some ways it sounded as if they had got together and discussed it in detail. It shook me rigid, but I suppose I've never realised how commonplace divorce has become. The trouble is, I can't really believe it is happening to me.

I did my best, a pretty poor one I fear, but they all looked relieved to get something even semi-definite although it seemed very hazy to me. God knows how we've brought them up; I was taken aback when Des cooly said, "We would like to know if you think marriage is on the way out and if so, what is going to replace it?" I'm sure at 15, I would not and could not, in the middle of so much turmoil, have begun a philosophical discussion! I muttered

122

something about marriage being the best thing going as long as it worked, and then, you won't believe it, they all piled in with views on women's lib, better not to have kids, a roving life for Des, and so much rubbish that I let it flow over me.

One hopes, at least, that it dispersed some of their anxiety and helped them sort out a torrent of mixed-up ideas. Karen's "Men are hopeless" and Julia's "Men, maybe, but not boys" brought a laugh and eased things a bit. We had spent two and a half hours talking and I was exhausted but if I hadn't closed it down they would have gone on! Des excelled himself by asking for a date for the next meeting and not to be late with items for the agenda!

I really would be so grateful for more on how to handle the kids. To-night was a real eye-opener and I'm glad at least you've taught us to value good communication, even if it is a bit shattering! . . . "

The Choice Of Subjects For A Forum

For the forum to be a success, subjects chosen and permitted for discussion need careful scrutiny. Only problems affecting the family as a whole should be accepted; those relating to an individual are barred.

In the last example the husband and wife 'owned' the problem of their relationship and decision to separate, but the effects of the break-up related to the whole family and so were eligible for a forum discussion, so long as no personal attacks were made. Mother's wish to take on a job is not a forum decision, but how the job affects the family and how to organise for this is a family matter. Mother's, or anyone else's taste in clothes is their own business and they would mightily resent family discussion on this topic.

How a child keeps his own room is his concern as is how much and what he eats within the choices set by the cook! Homework is a child's problem. No one can force a child to work or learn. Getting homework done is not a forum matter but having a place and peace and quiet to work in, is. Choice of friends, length and style of hair, and spending pocket-money are all personal and so not acceptable on the forum agenda. The family budget and how it is shared are clearly suitable for discussion, with parents retaining the right of final decision.

An individual's life-style and values are his own concern. The family meeting may air general views on the subject but they need to be strictly impersonal, even by implication, and no rules on behaviour can be laid down. Direct warnings on the dire consequences of 'disapproved' behaviour involving drugs, smoking, pre-marital sex and vandalism will usually fall on deaf ears and so are not suitable for the agenda. However, open discussion on such subjects can develop naturally and give an opportunity for parents to influence behaviour and values.

In 'one-to-one' situations

Compromise solutions sometimes cannot be found. This is more common in 'one-to-one' confrontations where one person sticks his toes in and for some reason is not secure enough to give and take but insists on all or nothing. This sort of situation often concerns a child in his mid-teens whose parent is determined to have his own way because he thinks that it is in the best interest of his child and that he is in the best position to judge. The trouble is he has no way of forcing the issue when, as so often happens, the child simply refuses to accept his judgment.

When a child insists on going his or her way and is totally unwilling to come to any compromise then the indications are that all is not well with family relationships. There is probably a lack of warmth and there also may be emotional hunger of some kind. In such cases parents have no alternative but to start from scratch and use all the skills that have been described for reducing tension and at the same time fortifying the emotional needs of feeling loved, building up self-esteem and having fun.

By the mid-teens, progress may be slow and difficult, especially if all these have been neglected over a long time. But however difficult, it is better than the alternative, which is to rant and rave and make hollow threats. In the end the young person may have to learn the hard way by his mistakes, but at least, when the chips are down, he will be fortified by the knowledge of his parents' love and support. If communication has been kept open the blows can be softened and the inner emotional reserves of strength to face them can be built up. An example may help drive this point home:

Joanna, aged 16, often stays out very late with a boyfriend whom her parents judge to be unreliable and unsuitable. This presents a problem that all their efforts at making pleas, Responsive Listening and seeking a compromise have failed to resolve. What options remain open to them? It is worth pointing out that the choice of boyfriend is entirely Joanna's problem and needs to be left to her. If her choice is attacked she will feel justifiably resentful; parents will only cement the relationship if they attack it. If on the other hand they are able to bring themselves to keep quiet and invite the boy into the home background, they can discuss with Joanna — without antagonism — any differences that show up, giving her the chance to pinpoint his unsuitability for herself.

When a child is driven to be loyal in the midst of a romance, any criticism or dire warning will fall on deaf ears. Of course there is always the outside possibility that the parents' judgment may prove to be wrong and their fears groundless, so in the end all can be happily resolved.

Apart from her choice of friend, her late hours also present a problem and that is a legitimate cause for concern by parents who are responsible for her safety; so the problem is a family one. If Joanna is unwilling to come to any compromise over the hours she keeps then her parents need to look at their overall relationship with their daughter, and, if need be, start from the beginning and build it up. Communication must be kept going at all costs, as once this is lost, so is any hope of further influence or control. The child, after hotly putting her own case, will not be inclined to continue the dialogue with her parents unless they can convince her that they genuinely wish to understand her point of view.

With younger children who say 'NO' and seem prepared to stick to it come what may, the problem is easier. First, because the reason for this stubborn refusal can usually be found if enough trouble is taken to search for it and once identified it can usually be dealth with. Second, the child is young enough for any threats used to be carried out. For example: "If you don't eat what is in front of you then you must realise that is all there is". or "If you don't help with your share of the washing-up you will have to be prepared to eat off your dirty plate".

If all the usual tension-release methods, promise of reasonable rewards and the action-related consequences fail to break the 'NO' pattern, then expert help needs to be sought.

In family forum situations

As in the case of 'one-to-one' confrontations, so the family forum does not always work smoothly. Occasionally there may be refusal to participate, excuses over forgetting to attend, or a walk-out in the middle of a meeting. Every child and parent will at some time or other come across the reaction of "No, I won't agree", "No, I think it is unfair", "I don't see why I should, and I won't change my mind". At times when these sorts of statements are heard there may be general agreement on postponing the meeting, shelving the problem for the moment, and giving everyone time to cool down and have second thoughts. Everybody experiences bouts of bad temper and unreasonable stubbornness; trying to force an issue under such circumstances is useless, whereas given the time, the problem under dispute can be seen in better proportion and resolved with less difficulty.

If at following meetings failure to find compromise solutions persists, then certain questions have to be considered and the deep-seated reasons for the stalemate found. The first question that needs to be asked concerns the whole idea of a family forum; has it merely been given lip-service agreement? Has it been introduced too suddenly and without careful enough preparation? Does it seem as if parents have imposed the idea on the young? Are authoritarian methods used by parents so there is a scepticism about the whole idea? Children may even believe it to be a new way for parents to enforce their ideas.

To rectify this situation, or better still to prevent it ever happening, a full discussion on the pros and cons of a forum needs to take place, the children saying how they feel it should be run and a clear statement being made that it is not a means for parents to pass on their ready-made solutions. 'One-to-one' experience in problem solving is the easiest way to try the idea out and if it works, the family meeting is likely to get off to a better start.

In face of failure other questions need answering: Was the first meeting a success? Was it a fairly lighthearted affair? Was the original idea to start a family forum made when things were running smoothly or when a crisis was looming? One can decide from the answers to these questions whether the forum got off on the right foot or not. If mistakes have been made they need to be aired and children allowed to say if they would prefer their family problems to be solved in another way.

Failure may also arise from a child fearing he may be criticised, put in the hot seat and in the end made to give way. He may feel pressured and so rebel and refuse to cooperate. Perhaps insufficient care has been taken to avoid personal tastes and values being discussed in the forum, and if so, a re-appraisal is needed as to who owns a particular problem. Any problem that is not the concern of the family as a whole needs to be dropped. Reassurance and responsive listening can lessen the fear of attack, especially if the parent or child feels free to express his own point of view about it. Many families find it a good idea to vet problems coming up for discussion and veto anything that is personal to an individual. For instance take the problem: "Shall we or shall we not decide, as a family, against smoking?". This can be a barbed question, particularly if only one member happens to smoke. No one would be surprised if he or she walked out.

Another reason for failure is that someone may still think in terms of winning or losing, rather than in terms of compromise. Usually the danger of losing is unacceptable so refusal to participate is a way of avoiding the issue. Sometimes there is a fear that part of the family will gang up against the rest, such as adults versus the young or boys versus girls; the discussion then is no longer fair. Ganging up needs to be nipped in the bud as soon as it appears.

When one child refuses to cooperate, even when the forum idea has been going well for some time, then patient reassurance about personal problems not being attacked is the only way to try and bring the wayward child back into the fold. No one can be forced to attend or agree to a particular solution. When there is disagreement it is better to release tension by allowing resentment and fear to be talked about openly.

As has been said so often, the sooner children share in solving family problems as a group, the sooner the idea of give and take becomes accepted. Meetings become something to look forward to as a part of everyday living. In some families it may be the parents leading a busy life who fail to respond.

They may be the ones to get slack and make excuses. They may have to be kept up to the mark by the young who genuinely enjoy feeling they have a say in family matters. If one member still refuses to participate after every effort has been made to hear their point of view, then it has to be accepted without making the individual feel he is being ostracised. This simple comment: "Do come along when you feel like it. We will really miss not hearing what you have to say", gives the right tone.

The family notice-board

Various reasons have been put forward why the family forum may fail. The reasons may be too deep-seated to be resolved, in which case the family may prefer to act as a collection of individuals.

Even if this is accepted and the forum ruled out, some coordination and cooperation is essential in any family. In this case the family notice-board can fill the gap. It can become the focal point around which the family organises itself and can act as a link between each member of the family and the others. It can, of course, be used as an addition to the forum idea.

A piece of softboard, 2ft x 2ft, set up at a convenient height and place for all the family, will be enough to get things going. When children are young it can be used to display their first efforts at pictures or crafts. Parents can use the board for reminders of appointments, social engagements and phone messages.

As the children grow older and life becomes more complex so the notice-board grows in importance and value. There are library books to return, music lessons to remember, dentist's and doctor's appointments, sharing of transport and sports equipment, changes of meal times to meet special needs, dates when friends or relations are calling and perhaps staying. All can be recorded on the notice-board. In this way all are kept informed and the board soon becomes as essential as the cooker.

In the teens, when life becomes really busy, the board will almost certainly need extending. The board itself cannot solve any problems but, by its existence, it encourages members of the family to think in terms of mutual assistance and interaction. It can sow the seeds of solving problems together and so can be a natural forerunner to setting up a forum.

It can also be a valuable addendum to the forum. For example, one sceptic said, "I don't see how anybody remembers any of the decisions we have made or any of the complicated share-outs". The answer came readily, "Look on the notice-board! They're all there, dates, agenda, decisions, the lot. If we go to all the trouble of discussing and deciding things then it is worth being sure no one slides out of agreements because they say they forgot!"

127

Taking decisions should not be confused with reaching agreed compromise solutions in face of conflict. Many family decisions need to be taken that involve no confrontation at all. Some family decisions may come up in the family forum, some may have to be taken on the spot as they cannot wait, and some will be discussed informally. However decisions are made, they can be of vital importance to the smooth running of a family. Good decisions do a lot to keep down hassle, bad ones can create chaos. So it is useful to be aware of the difficulties and how to avoid them. A few suggestions follow as many of us have to learn the skill before we can pass it on to our children.

Any decision which involves a number of options needs time for looking into the background; hasty decisions often prove to be ill-considered ones. When making a decision, the future as well as the present have to be taken into account. Children are apt to settle for the easy option, only considering the immediate effects. If the idea is a new one then rash decisions may be reached that will not stand the test of time and later give rise to protests about being pushed into it or not realising all that it meant!

Children will be more highly motivated to enter into a discussion with concentration if they know that decisions that follow are likely to make sense for ALL the family not just the grown-ups. If they do not feel this, but suspect they are entering into a win or lose struggle, they will tend to argue rather than discuss and decisions will be that much harder to reach. Emphasis on "What is best for us all" helps any decision-making discussion.

Decisions, once the implications have been fully explored, need to be finalised. No loose ends should be left. Otherwise the same old toing and froing crops up time and again. For instance, the use of the family car may involve who has priority over its use, the exceptions to this, who fills it with petrol and oil, who is finally responsible for servicing and so on. It is easy to see how endless rows and 'blaming the next chap' may occur if definite decisions are not taken on each and every aspect and then recorded.

There are various difficulties that arise in day-to-day decision making that differ from family to family. Some members of a family may be less efficient or less capable than others, who make them feel that their opinions hardly count. Care has to be taken to avoid this happening even to the extent of slowing the pace of the discussion to suit the least verbalised and most indecisive child. In other cases a child or adult will avoid ever committing himself to decide anything. This lack of self-confidence needs to be worked on and efforts made to build up self-esteem during discussions.

Naturally there are some decisions which parents alone can make because the implications are too far-reaching for any but the older and more mature teenagers to grasp. If, however, from the start the family hear Mum and Dad discussing decisions together and making them jointly instead of some being Dad's and others Mum's, then this builds up their sense of togetherness when family interests are involved. Children will always be happier over parental decisions when they know that they are joint ones and that Mum and Dad are fully behind them. For example, parents may decide to send their son to boarding school. He, and his brothers and sisters, will probably have a lot to say about it but as availability of money, future career and quality of education to suit that particular individual are involved, the final decision rightly rests with the parents.

The rest of the family will accept the parental ruling much more readily and with much less anxiety if they sense that both Mum and Dad are fully involved and have decided together and that it is not just Dad pushing his son into following in his own footsteps. In any discussion, Mum's support of Dad's decision is important and it needs to be based on fact and not to be just a case of going along with him. For instance, Mum may contribute the idea that she knows how well Dad enjoyed and benefited from boarding-school and so is behind his wish to give his son the same chance.

A person's right to take part in family decision-making should not be dependent on his proven ability always to make good decisions. In fact if an option, put forward by a child, should go wrong then "I told you so" should be avoided at all costs. Rather, support needs to be given and confidence restored by a "We all make mistakes sometimes" and "We were all party to the decision" attitude.

Just because a person happens to be the expert or is best informed in one particular field this does not give him the right, or obligation, to make all decisions in that quarter. Dad is hot on finance and holds the purse-strings but the rest of the family would question that this gives him the right to choose where the family goes on holiday. For the same cost many options would be open. Mum does the cooking but everyone wants a share in deciding what sort of food they will enjoy. Don is good with bikes but heaven forbid that he will decide what kind Michael is going to have. Sheila is a sports fan but it does not give her priority over which sports programmes will be turned on for family viewing.

Decision-making, whether between parents or in a family forum can make the difference between a mediocre family life in which each does the best for himself, or a more meaningful, integrated existence where there is an awareness of everyone's needs. The idea that most of us want to pass on to our children is the importance of deciding what is for the common good and how a particular option affects all the family.

Finally, parents need to keep a careful watch on how their decision-making works in practice. Is it fair, is it just, does it take account of everyone's wants and views? This is what will be picked up by the children and no amount of telling them how it OUGHT to be done will have the same impact as practising what is preached.

"Do what Pa says, not what Pa does" is a sure recipe for hassle!

CHAPTER 14: A Shoulder To Lean On

Our Reluctance To Seek Help Over Emotional Problems

None of us likes to admit failure in dealing with family relationships or with a child's behaviour problems. Somehow failure of this kind seems to reflect discredit on the family. We all dislike the idea of others pointing the finger at us, hinting that we are incompetent, that any mess we are in is our own fault or shows up a weakness in our character. It follows then, that if we fail to face up to our problems, we certainly will not ask for help to solve them.

The truth of the matter is that life becomes a hassle for most people at one time or another. We are all in the same boat. Anyone may have to face a total impasse in their relationships, whether with children or their mate. Heredity, physical make-up, emotional predisposition as well as environmental and unforeseen circumstances, are all uncannily disrespectful of personal relationships.

There are very few parents who fail to do their best for their children or do not wish for satisfying relationships for themselves. Why then, are most of us so reluctant to seek help when the going gets rough? Why do we so often wait until things are absolutely desperate? After all, we are ready to fly to the social services if we lose our job or money gets very short. We do not hesitate to go to the doctor if anyone in the family gets ill and we certainly feel no sense of shame attached to such a visit. None of us sits worrying until we are tied up in emotional knots if our child is in pain or has a high temperature; we act quickly and take no chances. We willingly face the possibility of our GP suggesting that we are fussing or that it might be our fault. Is physical health any more of a hazard than unhappiness and emotional upset?

For some reason shame and fear of blame seem to be the main factors that colour our attitudes and stop us from accepting that hassle and stress are not matters for moral judgment. Perhaps we are too slow to acknowledge the fact that emotional disturbances can be as far-reaching in their effects as physical illness; that the need for expertise, prevention and first aid are equally urgent and necessary in dealing with either physical or emotional problems.

Ways To Overcome Our Prejudices

First of all, we have to face up to our reluctance, real or imaginary. We seldom blame ourselves if we get physically ill even if we have been careless. We tend to think of it as bad luck and so do those around us. But social censure, damaging to our self-esteem, seems to surround us as soon as we become emotionally upset. So much so that many people go to great lengths to make excuses, to justify the way they feel, to deny the existence of any emotional problems and so refuse to get help. This solves nothing and can land a person in a lot of unhappiness. If, when looking on from the side-lines, a close friend suggests that we try to get some help and we find ourselves beginning to make excuses, then a red warning light should flash! When this happens, the time has almost certainly come to take our courage in both hands and make a positive move to get some help or support.

The second way we can break down our prejudices is to allow ourselves to appreciate the extent of the relief that will come the moment our problem is shared. Finally there is the comfort that someone who is not too close to the problem may see a solution that we have failed to find. Often, we really try to sort things out for ourselves, but without support, sympathy and understanding our resolve weakens and we slip back to where we started. To illustrate this there follows part of a tape recording from a young woman who appreciated the advantage of finding support: " . . . It was my husband who first suggested my trying the counselling service. He reminded me of all my failures to get slim until I got help from a weight-watching group. He's right. I couldn't go it alone and found I was slipping into bad old habits. Perhaps it is the same over our problems with Anne. We have had a stab at doing what we thought was correct but things have gone from bad to worse and now we don't know what to think or which way to turn. I wish to goodness we hadn't delayed as we are all in a bigger mess than a month ago. Thank you for replying so promptly. I didn't like to say how desperately we needed advice . . . ".

Once prejudices have been overcome about asking for help, then we need to be clear when help is needed. We need to know, as precisely as possible, what sort of problems with our children call for expert advice and which we should be able to cope with ourselves. This information follows.

How To Know When Help Is Needed

Like the mother who sent the tape appealing for help, any parent who begins to feel overwhelmed is definitely in need of help. They can only benefit by telling someone about their difficulties and seeking advice on how to begin tackling them.

Sometimes the need is not as clear-cut as this. A parent may suspect his child is going through a difficult but passing phase and not want to make too much fuss about it. Genuine concern can never be classed as fussing and if the whole situation is getting the parent down, then advice and reassurance will bring relief.

It is easy to recognise if a child needs expert help. He does so when his distressing or anti-social behaviour persists to the extent that it disturbs the community or disrupts family life. This can happen if, for example, a child is excessively and persistently aggressive, fearful, unable to relate to others, suffers repeated nightmares or displays developmental or speech difficulties. These, and other excessive forms of behaviour, leave no doubt that the child is in need of expert help. It has to be emphasised that the behaviour has to be so persistent that it could not possibly be passed off as just another phase of normal development.

For example, if a child of 10 years still wets the bed, masturbates openly or is excessively disobedient or uncooperative, this clearly falls outside any normal awkward phase. In the same way it is obvious that teenagers who show signs of addiction to drugs or alcohol, who are patently delinquent or markedly depressed and withdrawn, are in need of expert help.

There is another form of behaviour that parents need to be especially warned about. This is the sort that causes no trouble or concern and so can easily go unrecognised as a problem of any importance. These types of problems will be described in greater detail in order to alert parents to the insidious dangers of some of the less easy to recognise areas where outside help is definitely needed.

The "Hard To Recognise" Problems

So what about these signs and symptoms that are hard to recognise, which can slip by unnoticed or possibly be even welcomed or encouraged? The least that parents can do is to learn about these "hard to spot" types of behaviour and so be better equipped to recognise them before they develop in more serious and stressful ways. Some examples follow:

1) *The over-shy child*

Unlike the excessively withdrawn child, the shy child is excused, protected and often welcomed as being sensitive in contrast to those who push themselves to the front and show off.

Persistently shy children appear submissive, say comparatively little and, if given the choice, isolate themselves from others. Ordinary anger and aggression are something they cannot tolerate and they tend to cry for very little reason, often being nicknamed 'cry baby'.

An over-shy child avoids unfamiliar adults and prefers younger children as playmates. When approached they hang their heads and answer in monosyllables, if at all. To be the centre of attention is agony! Usually they cling to mother or father but as they grow older their lack of any really warm relationship means they have few friends and live lonely lives. As younger children other people often talk for them. "Oh, she would love to come" mother answers for Hilda when she refuses to reply to a spoken invitation. While meaning to be kind her mother is aiding and abetting her shyness.

No one notices that shy children, normal in physical and mental development, fail to take any initiative and if demands are made on them that they feel are too great they keep quietly to themselves, read, watch TV or listen to music.

A mother sent this tape asking for advice about Jenny, aged 14: "Jenny has never been any trouble, she is quiet, shy and sensitive. Everyone in the family feels protective towards her. Phillip and I felt all this was just her personality. We recognised that she was different from us as we are both outgoing people. I suppose in the back of my mind I felt that she wanted to be different, but somehow we never worried about her. For the first time I am concerned and upset by the fact that she has no friends, won't go out except for walks by herself and sometimes seems very depressed. When she started talking less and less we had a word with her teacher who says that Jenny is never any trouble but is often listless and seems to be in a world of her own. This is getting to be unnatural and we both sense something may be wrong, but I must confess it is nothing sudden. I think if we had been aware of it, the same sort of behaviour has been going on since she was about 5 . . .".

This is quite a common story, and although it was better late than never, Jenny could have been helped far more easily if her withdrawal had been spotted earlier. Normally shy people feel afraid when they meet new people or situations but this passes once they become familiar with their surroundings. Sooner or later they begin to make friends and enjoy the company of others. On the other hand, the over shy child never seems to build up enough confidence to relate to people outside the immediate family and the shy behaviour shows up and persists in every facet of his existence. This sort of child is calling for professional help.

2) *The over-protected child*

The wish to be protected often goes unnoticed. Parents easily convince themselves that clinging dependence is flattering. The lisping speech, the coy smile, the warm affection shown by such dependent children are all endearing characteristics. A mother may get impatient at not being able to leave her child, also at his refusal to eat unless fed, to dress unless helped or to play by himself, but she accepts it because it feeds her natural wish to feel wanted and to be the centre of her child's life. Many only children and delicate children develop these tendencies, but any child who demands the same sort of attention he had as a baby can develop this type of behaviour.

Parents can themselves unwittingly encourage dependence and restrict independence, tying children to their apron strings in many subtle ways. Often such parents have an unspoken fear of letting their chicks out to face the big bad world. In other cases the child's every whim is catered for, he has no training in facing frustration, decisions are made for him, his whole life is organised for him and temptation is never put in his way.

The trouble is that parents often refuse to recognise what is happening and do not realise that their wish to protect is no answer to the preparation needed for the knocks life will certainly bring. Enjoying 'staying a baby' affects adult sex-life and future relationships, stultifies the imagination and initiative and when suddenly, for any reason, there is no one to lean on, the shock of all props disappearing is just too great to bear. Serious breakdown is a real possibility because adaptation is poor. An unsuccessful love affair or circumstances that bring about sudden separation, can trigger off serious depression or stupid immature rebellion.

After reading this perhaps some mothers and fathers may get a flash of insight and see what they have been doing without meaning to. They may recognise that their concern has been turned by their child into an essential prop. If this is so, then before going to the opposite extreme and throwing their unprepared child to the wolves, they might seek expert help and perhaps look for support from all the family to put matters right.

3) *Over-good children*

This type of child is every mother's dream come true! Unfortunately being excessively well-behaved is not natural. The child who is like this is usually hiding aggression and anxiety. He is not a spontaneously happy, mischievous youngster. He will usually worry if he is not clean, orderly, obedient, well-mannered and helpful. He lacks normal devilment and shows little sign of healthy high spirits or carefree abandon. He is gentle and kind, nonassertive, unselfish and spends a lot of his time thinking up small acts that will please. He is far too nice!

The whole attitude of this child is centred upon being appreciated and doing the right thing. All children of this type has one thing in common: their mothers think they are God's gift to harrassed mums but they complain that their child always seems listless and tired. They often go to their doctor afraid that their child has some hidden disease, or is in need of a tonic. Their concern is not misplaced but the disease is not physical and the tonic needed is not out of a bottle. The fatigue comes from the sheer continuous effort of holding in and denying normal aggression. They dare not show their own bad feelings.

Few parents are capable of even believing that there can be anything wrong with such paragons of virtue, but discerning teachers spot them, and when they do, it is wise for parents to heed their warnings.

With family cooperation and sound expert advice, help can be given easily and quite quickly. Once the child is able to face in himself what he has been at such pains and effort to hide, the likelihood is that future adaptation will be quite normal. The fear that one day the cork will pop and the explosion bring great danger and unhappiness can soon be dispelled. When no action is taken, however, the following remarks could well apply: "Well, would you ever have thought John could behave like that? It's so out of character. I've always thought of him as the kindest, nicest sort of person and just look what he has done. It's unbelievable!". This is just the type of 'explosion' that can occur. For many parents it might be a comfort to know that "Too good is not always very happy", and no counsellor would show any surprise at being consulted about such a paragon of virtue.

Problems We All Face

We have dealt with the obvious and the not-so-obvious cases when parents, and more particularly their children, are showing signs that they are in need of expert help.

There is a different set of problems that are not so serious but which produce nagging anxiety and tend to get parents down. These are the problems which arise in the normal ups and downs of bringing up children.

The trouble is often short-lived, just a phase that passes, but while it lasts life can be very trying. For instance, consider the worrying times with a first baby, especially if he cries incessantly; then the period of the terrible 2's, 3's and 4's when children assert themselves and learn to manipulate their parents; then later the teenage years which are always a fairly traumatic period when parents have to untie the umbilical cord and watch the young suffer mistakes and heartaches. Any of these periods are the most likely times for parents to be tested and tried. Some reassurance and first-aid type of assistance can be supportive and help to get through a difficult patch.

Although young children can drive parents to near-distraction, it is the teenage years that cause the most anxiety. This is especially true if communication is not good and warm relationships have cooled off. Most parents know that they have to be on the look-out for signs of trouble. These show through exaggerated teenage moods: being too way-out or rebellious, too self-critical, too dependent on their peer group, having too few friends or being over-excitable or depressed too often. There may be too much interest in sex or too little, too much day-dreaming or too little effort at school work. Any or all of these moods can come and go, often leaving parents fairly uptight.

Then there is the never-ending stream of decisions that have to be made. How strict should we be? What stand should we take over morals and values? Can we enforce our demands? How do we encourage independence and yet guard against its abuse? Is it to be the Pill or not the Pill? How much freedom should we allow for experimentation in modern distractions? These are only a few of the anxiety-provoking decisions that face parents today. All this is on top of the pressures of a busy life and ups and downs with a marriage partner. No wonder some tend to wilt under the strain! It is at times like these that parents can find support and relief by taking advantage of some of the first-aid facilities which will be described.

'First-Aid' and self-help facilities

A number of alternatives exist that fall into the self-help category. The media do a great deal to help in this direction through the number of first-rate courses on child-rearing that appear on television and radio. Then there is a mass of helpful reading matter available. Enquiries about books and pamphlets can be made to the Health Education Council or to any public library.

The subjects covered by this kind of literature are very wide-ranging, and whatever the problem, it is likely to have been dealt with in depth. If continuous hassle happens to be the problem then a book like this might help parents to teach themselves the various skills that will promote more harmony. Having a definite goal of, say, improving communication or finding agreed solutions can bring a sense of purpose and direction that may help in what seems to be an impasse. Merely working as a husband and wife team, by deciding together on a definite plan to meet a problem, can also bring relief.

Another form of self-help is to learn how to relax when a situation is getting one uptight. Special audio-tapes are available which claim to induce a more relaxed attitude, both mentally and physically. Other ways of encouraging relaxation may, for some, be found through transcendental meditation or yoga, whilst for those with a deep-seated religious faith, prayer can bring extra strength and peace of mind. Sometimes the saying "A problem shared is a problem halved" can be put to the test with advantage by confiding in a trusted friend whose understanding and reassurance may help lessen the feeling of panic.

Quite often outside help is needed only because the will to help ourselves is lacking. When this is the case there are a number of options open. Many towns have 'Walk In' centres where trained social workers or psychologists are available to give help. Many parishes too have a counselling service, which may or not have trained counsellors available. The social services make provision for health visitors to call on mothers with new babies or toddlers. Health centres often set up support groups and courses for families with temporary stressful problems. The family GP, if liked and trusted, can give great support although their time is often limited. Unless one member of the practice specialises in emotional family problems it may be necessary to be referred to a Walk-In centre.

Citizens' Advice Bureaux can usually give the whereabouts of nearby Walk-In centres and support groups. These support groups are run voluntarily and cover a wide range of problems. They include groups for lonely mothers, single parents, teenage problem groups, Alcoholics Anonymous and the Samaritans, who can be telephoned at any time of the night or day; groups for divorcees, hard-done-by fathers, married partners of homosexuals, parents

137

of handicapped children and many more. The mere existence of so many groups is a measure of their popularity and usefulness. People with common problems can derive great help, support and solace from each other.

In some cases a minister of church, a school-teacher or a youth centre leader can be approached for temporary support and first-aid help. Naturally the success of this first aid will depend upon how well the parent likes and respects the individual concerned, how capable they are and how much time they are willing to give.

The Social Services will usually arrange for a social worker to visit on request, but in some areas these services are stretched to the limit. Where this applies, little effective help can be given. Because of this, together with a wish to remain anonymous, many parents have turned to newspaper or magazine columnists who offer advice. Such an approach may bring a useful reply but no long exchange of advice or therapy can be expected.

Another source of help lies in the 'Tape Services' which are becoming available. The parent sends a tape-recording explaining his problem to a professional counsellor who sends a personal reply by the same medium, giving advice and where necessary, asking follow-up questions. This back-and-forth communication can continue for as long as necessary. It does avoid the necessity for appointments and leaving home. The parent is able to release tension by talking freely about his problem when things are at their worst and without any delay beyond his own choosing.

Professional help over more serious problems

When there is a more serious problem that calls for help then the family doctor is often the most accessible person. He can refer parents to the appropriate specialist or advise them on the most suitable facilities that are available. The GP may refer them to a hospital outpatient department or a health centre or suggest a child guidance unit, a school psychological service or a marriage guidance service. He should know of all the various units available or at least be able to tell parents where to go to find out.

The family doctor or GP is not always the answer. One mother had the following comments to make: "It's OK for you — you say your GP is an angel, but mine — phoo! Medically he is terribly efficient and up-to-date, and that's why I went to see him originally, but he is so cold, unsympathetic and prickly that nothing would induce me to confide in him over personal worries. I'd either find myself whisked off to Psychiatric Outpatients, or brushed off as one of those who wastes his valuable time!". It takes all kinds to make a world and doctors are no exception. A change of GP might be the best answer.

Some parents find the Citizens' Advice Bureaux a great help in giving information about all the services available in the district. Most CAB's are extremely helpful and very understanding. They will give information as to how to get referred if the GP is unable to help. In some health centres and outpatients, people can just walk in and they will be referred to the right department. The same goes for the Social Services if a person with enough time to spare can be cornered!

In some parts of the country Child and Family Centres and School Psychological Services have long waiting-lists but anyone with an urgent problem can usually be seen quite quickly.

There are many private services which naturally have to be paid for. A general practitioner will, on request, suggest a consultant psychiatrist, a psychologist or psychotherapist. There are any number of experts in different types of therapy. These include group therapy, behavioural therapy, cognitive therapy, psycho-drama, educational and occupational therapists, vocational experts, remedial teachers and educational consultants. The service that provides counselling services through the use of tape-recording has already been mentioned.

In some instances, to use these services, a parent will need to be referred, but in others they can make a direct approach. It is wise to get a recommendation or consult a GP rather than rely on advertisements in the newspaper. A great number of these private consultants are fully qualified in their particular field, but as in most other areas, there are always some unqualified operators who, if they are unscrupulous, can lead patients 'up the garden path'!

For this reason the question may be asked: "If I use a private service how do I select a suitable one?". If your GP cannot help then the only way is to work on the recommendation of someone else you trust. In very general terms, psychiatrists are medically qualified doctors. Psychologists, some psychoanalysts, psychotherapists and counsellors are not, but are highly trained in their specialities. All of them may handle many different types of therapy but only psychiatrists and other medically qualified practitioners can give prescriptions.

There are many capable shoulders on which to lean when we are faced with serious problems that call for expert help. In addition, there is a wide range of facilities that can bring much needed support in times of stress. The choice is there but whether or not we ask for the help that is available is up to us. "I only wish I had gone for help sooner", is a commonly heard cry.

The wish always to appear successful and to be able to manage on our own, is one we all share, but for many it is a pipe dream. Reality, not dreams, is what counts when we begin to feel life is getting on top of us or we see our children getting uptight.

Is It Ever Too Late To Be Helped?

One couple expressed their concern like this: "We have accepted the fact that our problem (Sean taking drugs) is seen as not quite 'respectable'. We are ready to accept blame if it is justified. We know it is foolish but we are horrified at the thought of neighbours gossiping when they get to know that we ourselves are now getting psychiatric help. All this is hard enough to take, but our real concern is the thought that we may have left it too late to be of any help to Sean. We despair that the damage done may be beyond repair".

The answer is straightforward. Any parents who are prepared to make the sacrifices and face the embarrassment they say they will feel once they seek expert help, are likely to sustain the effort that will be needed to solve their problem. This may well mean starting from scratch and opening their minds to a completely new approach so as to build a warmer relationship and re-open communication with their child. They may ask: "But how will our child react to this new approach after so many years? He is now in his mid-teens and has become used to something quite different. Will he ever accept the change? How do we start? He refuses to discuss anything or confide at all. Relationships are less than cool and he is only interested in what suits him".

Even in the face of all these difficulties, teenage children can be brought to accept changes in relationships. This is more likely if they can be persuaded to see the changes as beneficial. No new approach can be forced on anyone but it is unlikely that a disturbed child will be enjoying his discontent, so there will be a chance that he will be amenable to change. Even if he pretends that life is good he will certainly have doubts about his self-image and so will tend to grasp at any chance to build it up.

This build-up of self-esteem could be the catalyst leading towards better things all round. But without meaningful communication and warmth little will be accomplished. To achieve these two essentials may mean a long job starting all over again learning about emotional needs, learning the skills that go towards keeping stress down and communication open. The later help is sought the more this new knowledge will have to be applied with faith, perseverance and above all, patience. During this time of rehabilitation, when there is a long, hard and uncertain road ahead, new skills to learn, set-backs to face, we should not hesitate to call for the support and the guidance that is always available. It is likely to bring comfort and new hope.

140

CHAPTER 15: The Family And The Community

This book has described a different approach to discipline. It has concentrated on how parents can encourage their children to be cooperative, caring people. The methods and skills needed to do this are very different from those used in putting across the old 'Do as I say and do it at once!' demands which people associate with discipline. The approach is equally different from the 'Do as you please' system associated with permissiveness. Neither of these well tried ways to decrease hassle and confrontation has succeeded.

At present we are surrounded by the anti-social behaviour of some youngsters who do not seem to understand what the word discipline means. The least excuse and they join in rioting, football hooliganism, set fires, mug and steal from helpless old people, attack their teachers and even hack people to death without any show of remorse. Today's children are tomorrow's adults and unless we tackle the problem it will escalate and the future of our society is pretty grim.

All this prophesying of doom has been heard down the ages, but here and now the horror is brought right into every home by the media and, as never before, we are unable to escape by pretending it only affects others. Our children are at risk because they are permeated with ideas of letting fly with their fists, making a quick buck, flouting authority and becoming insensitive to violence. Unemployment, poor living conditions, racial and religious prejudice may all add up to discontent and boredom but is spending billions on building an environmental utopia really the only answer? We would all like inner cities with tree-lined streets, cosy homes and steady jobs for everyone, but even if the money were found this would need many years to take effect and it is here and now that a remedy needs to be put into action.

There are plenty of ideas about alternative causes and about who is to blame. Some, say parents and teachers born in the 1950's and 1960's, think discipline a dirty word and are frightened as well as disinclined to assert control. Some think discipline is misused, with beatings and sadistic abuse being employed to a far greater extent than might be expected. Others maintain that for many parents their individual rights tend to take precedence over their duties and self-interest over concern for the young.

A group of discontented teenagers was asked what they thought lay behind their age group being so involved in violence. Oddly enough they minimised the effects of poor environment, the uncertainty over employment, poverty and boredom. These, they thought, were just an extra impetus to the wish to hit out and hit back. Instead they all emphasised that the wish to rebel would be far less strong if they got MORE UNDERSTANDING and more chance to MAKE DECISIONS for themselves. This is such old hat that we smile and take no notice. This message persists and comes again and again. One wonders if we adults will ever listen to it?

The authors of this book have tried to listen, and feel that there is one thing every parent can do here and now. Instead of walking away and turning their backs on the inevitable escalation of confrontation, they can take discipline in its original sense of 'learning' and take the job of the SOCIAL TRAINING of their youngsters very seriously.

It is never too late to begin this training. Although from birth to 6 years parental influence will be at its greatest, from 7 to 18 there is still plenty of chance to rectify mistakes and build new values. This is a vital, long as well as short term remedy which will not cost millions and can start right away in every home.

The message is urgent, not only for our own sakes because harmony is preferable to hassle in our homes, but because we parents have it in our hands to shape the sort of community our grandchildren will inherit. This is a challenge worth meeting. This book describes how to tackle this challenge by implanting ideas of caring and cooperating, showing the value of communication in settling differences and how to train children in decision-making from their earliest years.

It has not yet stressed the vital importance of how to help children become actively involved in their community. The present tendency towards isolation needs to be halted. This means, for many, a change in outlook. The home cannot merely be a refuge from unwelcome dangers and violence outside. Neighbours can no longer be viewed as nosey gossips, or teachers, social workers and police as people who interfere and are best avoided. Other people's children cannot only be seen as potential troublemakers whose rough behaviour, language and ideas may be infectious. These commonly-held views are not helping the present situation; in the long run the 'Blow you Jack — I'm all right' sort of stance increases tension and going it alone is a lonely and unrewarding path to tread.

For children, learning to integrate socially and to care for others, and getting on with all kinds of people and making friends at school, are an essential part of growing up. Children need to follow their parents' example in showing concern and helping others in the community. Most of all they need to taste the satisfaction of contributing outside the family as a follow-up to the charity they learn at home.

So many of us cannot find the time or the energy to get involved and instead cling to the imagined security of our own four walls. As an example the following true story gives food for thought. A social worker was questioning a 12 year old who had been knocked about by an intruder in his parents' absence:

"Why didn't you go for help?"

"Our neighbours can't be bothered with other people's business. We all keep ourselves to ourselves."

"Why didn't you go to a friend?"

"My gran and aunt both live too far away."

"What about the police?"

"My Dad says steer clear of the police."

What an indictment of city life today!

There is no doubt that the quality of life is enriched by the stimulation of rubbing shoulders with people who bring with them different outlooks, interests and abilities. None of us can afford not to be part of a community, especially when trouble strikes, nor can any family accept the services of other individuals without ever giving back something in return. Tension will rise in one way or another if there is no niche in the community into which we can fit and where we can feel relaxed and accepted.

Is this sense of belonging that brings peace of mind so hard to find? In the first place the myth of 'The less people I care about and mix with, the less chance of being let down' has to be exploded. The family that isolates itself, that is on the defensive, wrapped up in only its own concerns may never know the joy of helping and contributing in a wider sense. Experiencing this joy is something that all children can be offered. Friends and neighbours can be welcomed into the home to share family occasions. Children can be encouraged to give time for some kind of voluntary work without feeling that it is a punishment or something for which they expect a cash reward.

"But that is not possible where we live", was the excuse one family gave. In fact a quick survey of the street where they lived brought to light three pensioners who would have blessed anyone who offered to give even an hour's help in the house or garden. There was one single-parent family where the children got home before their mother and who would have eagerly welcomed some young company and a bit of supervision. There was a family with a badly-handicapped child where even a short break in the day would have lightened their very heavy burden. A few people in the street described themselves as lonely while one was positively depressed. There was a tendency for people to feel that their lonely plight was not their fault as they felt their neighbours should take the initiative. All were ready to talk and welcomed sincere concern as long as someone else made the first move!

Any family, regardless of colour, creed or standard of living, can at least attempt to put out the first hand of friendship. If the family relationships are good they will already have learned the value of taking the initiative if reconciliation is going to succeed. They will already know how often the first move to this end is reciprocated and the deep satisfaction that results.

In the community, the security of being able to rely on neighbours and being generally accepted and liked is reward enough for giving a helping hand to some needy individual or cause. Contributing or giving always builds up self-esteem whereas isolation asks for rejection and ostracism.

Everyone, to some extent, walks a tight-rope, balancing treasured privacy and independence against the satisfaction of feeling part of a community and looking outside the immediate family towards the needs of a wider circle of people. A man's house is his castle but to know true and lasting peace of mind it must never become a fortress.

143

INDEX